# What You Should Know About Homosexuality

Charles W. Keysor, editor, is the founder and present editor of
*Good News* Magazine. He received a B.S. degree in journalism
from the Medill School of Journalism, Northwestern Univer-
sity, Evanston, Illinois, and a M.Div. degree from Garrett
Theological Seminary, Evanston, Illinois. He has written the
following books: *Our Methodist Heritage, Living Unafraid,* and
*Come Clean!* He has also had articles published in *Christianity
Today, Christian Herald,* and other Christian magazines.

## ZONDERVAN
### PUBLISHING HOUSE

OF THE ZONDERVAN CORPORATION
GRAND RAPIDS, MICHIGAN 49506

# What You Should Know About Homosexuality

in • the Old Testament
in • the New Testament
in • church history
in • the physical and emotional
in • the courtroom
in • the church

Edited by Charles W. Keysor

WHAT YOU SHOULD KNOW ABOUT HOMOSEXUALITY
Copyright © 1979 by The Zondervan Corporation
Grand Rapids, Michigan


**Library of Congress Cataloging in Publication Data**

Main entry under title:
What you should know about homosexuality.

(Contemporary evangelical perspectives)
Includes bibliographical references and indexes.
1. Homosexuality—Moral and religious aspects.    2. Homosexuality
in the Bible.    I.   Keysor, Charles W.
HQ76.25.W5      261.8'34'157       79-21405
ISBN 0-310-38231-9

Printed in the United States of America


83   84   85   86   87   88 — 10   9   8   7   6   5   4

# Contents

# Foreword

Perhaps no other word causes more varied reactions among Christians than *homosexuality*. You could run the whole gamut of feelings and you would find that each one will fit someone: fear, revulsion, hostility, guilt, shame, panic, acceptance, understanding, compassion, and love.

But maybe the most common response today is confusion. Christians are hearing so-called authoritative voices saying homosexuality is either "a sin to be avoided," "a sickness to be treated," "a condition to be accepted," or "an alternate life style to be approved." For the first time in history some are even saying publicly, "Gay is good."

It is this widespread confusion that makes a book like this both important and relevant. The various authors are all outstanding in their respective fields and well equipped to give expert opinions, but it is their unanimous commitment to the authority of Scripture that makes them unique. This is more than simply citing as proof texts the usual passages dealing with homosexuality. An in-depth analysis of the total biblical world view of creation and human sexuality is made the foundation of their view. In this way the opinions of the behavioral scientists are weighed and answered in the light of God's Word and not the opposite as is being done in so many quarters today.

Most important of all, the authors have a genuine sense of pastoral concern for persons. Fidelity to God's design of sexual order does not lead to self-righteousness or "homophobia" but to loving and redemptive concern for those who need the healing fellowship of the church.

The ultimate aim of Christian knowledge is practical: to make us more loving and effective servants of our Lord, who never allowed compassion to compromise His highest principles or principles to lessen His deepest love. This book will help His disciples achieve that aim.

David A. Seamands
*Wilmore, Kentucky*

# Preface

The 1960s produced many challenges to traditional ideas and concepts. One of the most tenacious and controversial has been the effort to remove the stigma traditionally attached to homosexual practice. This aspect of the multifaceted "human rights" emphasis has grown steadily, both in power and visibility. During the latter 1970s, television, magazines, and newspapers have served increasingly as vehicles for the nontraditional viewpoint concerning homosexuals and homosexuality.

Psychology, psychiatry, law, education, politics, and other fields have become embroiled. It has been inevitable that religion would also be involved, for the Judeo-Christian tradition has been the main fountainhead of belief that homosexuality constitutes a perversion of the divinely appointed relationship between the two sexes.

The source of this view is the Bible, both Old and New Testaments. Therefore it has been inevitable that homosexual activists should seek to reinterpret the Bible. With surprising rapidity, during the 1970s, various reinterpretations of Scripture and Christian ethics have circulated within the more liberal "mainline" churches. From 1970 onward, pastors and church people have been confronted increasingly with reinterpretations that must be termed "radical" because they reach to the root meaning of human sexuality and of the Bible itself. Demands both subtle and strident are being made that people must be free to choose whichever sexual orientation they prefer. Being homosexual or heterosexual, we are told, is no more a matter of right or wrong than being blue-eyed or left-handed. Indeed, the only wrong, according to the reinterpretations, is interfering with anyone's right to be homosexual and, being homosexual, to hold any job, including that of pastor, priest, or rabbi.

Exponents of the traditional Judeo-Christian view of homo-sexuality have often entered this escalating controversy with responses coming more from emotion than solid understanding of their tradition. For this reason, the need for a book that presents seriously the traditional position on homosexuality has become increasingly evident. This was realized in 1975 by leaders of the "Good News Movement," a conservative, *ad hoc* group functioning as "a forum for Scriptural Christianity" within the United Methodist Church. Good News first entered the homosexual controversy in 1973, as it surfaced in America's second-largest Protestant denomination. Our involvement has been both political and theological, and out of this concern for the traditional position this book has emerged. I am grateful to Good News for financing the eighteen months of writing and research, to the contributors, to the publishers, and to my colleague, Mrs. Diane Knippers, who has shared so effectively the task of gathering and processing this material.

We hope this book will make a positive contribution by enabling all concerned to understand more accurately the traditional Judeo-Christian viewpoint.

We trust that this book will contribute both to an understanding of the immense problem of homosexuality and to an appreciation of the historic Judeo-Christian viewpoint as the only viable response to it.

Charles W. Keysor

# Two Testimonies

**1** As a lesbian and an elementary schoolteacher, I lived with the constant fear that someone would discover and reveal my chosen life style. The thought of the loss of my career and the disgrace and shame that that revelation would bring to my family made my life a nightmare.

I had committed my life to Christ when I was nine years old and by the time I was in junior high I regularly taught a Sunday school class in our small rural church. This active involvement in the church continued through my first years in college. However, I began to feel lost in the large college church and, seeking a more familiar rural setting, I began to work with, and be discipled by, two fellow students working in a church in a small farming community nearby.

Then I made a discovery—homosexuality is alive and well in the Christian church! The same person who discipled me as a growing Christian also "discipled" me as a lesbian. After two years of involvement in which I became more aware of the extent of homosexuality within local churches and Christian schools, I moved to another state and tried to leave my lesbian life style behind.

In search of help, I went to my pastor, sharing with him some of the reasons I had become gay, my desire to change, and my fear that I could not change. His response was an attempt to demonstrate that I could be aroused by a man. That attempt sent me back into the gay community. For the next five years I did not try to leave that security again.

But today I am no longer gay. God intervened through two people who really cared about me. They were a couple in my church who made themselves totally available. Their home was open to me at any time. They encouraged me and prayed for me and with me as I struggled to come to terms with the realization that my lesbian relationships always brought an immediate

11

sense of separation from God. Although my "Christian" friends had tried to tell me that I could be both Christian and lesbian, I knew that, for me at least, it just didn't work that way. Since I wanted to serve God, I knew I had to give up my lesbian life style; so I told God that in order to serve Him I would no longer be gay. To my dismay, I found I could not alter my life style. I could not say no to lesbian relationships.

After months of struggling to change myself, I came to the Lord completely defeated. I said, "I can't change. God, if You want me 'straight,' You'll have to change me." My deliverance wasn't instantaneous. For about a year I had to pray for strength every day not to make that phone call reopening my lesbian contacts. I failed a number of times during that year to use the strength available to me, but the Lord always brought me quickly to the place where I confessed my sin and relied again on His strength. Finally, I could say that I was no longer a practicing lesbian.

Three years later, during my first year of seminary, God accomplished another step in my deliverance. I realized that my major identity had been my lesbianism. That identity no longer fit; so I declared before God that because of His intervention in my life I was no longer gay. With the freedom from that label came a new dimension in my life. I am free to become the person God wants me to be because I no longer have expectations for myself that hinder His plans.

My friends in the gay community no longer seek me out. They are embarrassed by my presence in a group. My message to them both in word and action proclaims: "You can be free. You don't have to be gay forever. You can't change yourself, but God can change you. I know He can, because He changed me!"

**2** For years I doubted God's ability to deliver me from the oppression of homosexuality.

I accepted Christ as my Savior when I was twelve. Shortly after, Satan began to plague me with homosexual fantasies and to tell me that I could never be the totally surrendered Christian I longed to be. I desperately looked for someone I could trust to understand and help without condemning me, but I found no one. God has shown me now that the sin is not in being tempted but in yielding to the temptation, which I did not do until many years afterward.

I did not feel free to seek counseling from the church because many in the church had closed minds to this problem. Instead, I sought advice from unbelievers whose basic rule of life was, Do your own thing as long as you don't hurt anyone else. I didn't realize that this was the beginning of a great deception. God made me this way, I was told, and I was not to resist it.

The gay world, with its imitation of Christian love, accepted me unconditionally. The enemy worked cleverly to place me in a job that allowed me to live a double life. In my work I was associated with people in high places who led me further into active participation in the gay life. But I found myself caught in a web of deceit. I developed a sense of hopelessness so desperate that I considered suicide.

Then God led me to a fellowship of believers who helped me to experience the fullness of His Spirit. It was several years later, however, before I fully understood that the victory could not be complete until I confessed my problem to one or more members of the body of Christ. The beginning of my deliverance came when the Lord sent two special people into my life with whom I could be totally open. Through them I began to see God's unconditional love for me. I also began to sense God's hatred of sin because of its destructiveness within me.

After many years of being a practicing homosexual, I am no longer gay. My healing and deliverance are now realities for which I am deeply grateful. God brought me to the place where I was willing to surrender my entire life to Him completely— the good and the bad. He showed me that I could be committed without being surrendered but I could not be surrendered without be committed.

God has now called me to be an evangelist. He has commissioned me to share with those who are rejected and oppressed and to teach Christians how to deal with the problems of human sexuality. One of the greatest revelations to me is that the problem is not just homosexuality but sexuality in the broadest sense of that term.

Homosexuals desperately need the ministry of those who were formerly gay. So, I prayed for some time for God to show me a homosexual who had come out of the darkness—who had been delivered completely—and who could conduct a ministry to homosexuals. I felt that God's response was, "Russell, you're that man."

I counted the cost of making my past public. Fear and shame gripped me as I thought of sharing my trials and victory. I was especially concerned about how it would affect my Christian mother. In God's perfect timing, however, when I shared it with her, I found that she had already sensed my struggle and was led of God not to challenge or confront me but quietly to pray for me. She rejoices in my victory and is encouraging my ministry.

The Lord seemed to speak to me again, saying, "If I had healed you of cancer, you would be shouting it in the streets. I have healed you of another form of malignancy. Go and tell."

# 1

# The Old Testament and Homosexuality

The author is Professor of Old Testament at Asbury Theological Seminary, Wilmore, Kentucky. He received his A.B. degree from Taylor University, Upland, Indiana; his B.D. and Th.M. degrees from Asbury Theological Seminary; and his M.A. and Ph.D. degrees from Brandeis University. Dr. Oswalt has contributed articles to The Evangelical Quarterly and to the Zondervan Pictorial Encyclopedia of the Bible. He is a member of the Society of Biblical Literature, the Institute for Biblical Research, and the Wesleyan Theological Society.

## By John N. Oswalt

# Homosexuality

**in the Old Testament**
in the New Testament
in church history
in the physical and emotional
in the courtroom
in the church

**1** In any treatment of a complex ethical issue such as homosexuality, the essential question is, Is there a right or a wrong course? Some argue that right and wrong are relative, depending on the circumstances. Thus, *appropriate* and *inappropriate* would be better words, they say. This development is a result of discarding an objective ethical standard. Humans create their ethical standards, it is argued, and therefore those standards change, or ought to change, with changing times.

### THE AUTHORITY OF THE BIBLE

*Is There a Source of Moral Standards?*

But views such as these cause a problem. If we create the norms, if there are no standards of right and wrong outside of ourselves, then where did we get the idea of right and wrong? The concept of morality involves more than appropriateness or inappropriateness, as the concept of sin involves more than simple mistakes. Where did we get the idea of morality if there is no such thing as morality?

The Bible answers the question specifically. It says we have such a concept because we are made in the image of God. Therefore, what is out of keeping with His character is also out of keeping with our character, is destructive, and thus is wrong. Paul argues that even the pagans, who do not know the true God, recognize moral standards of a sort. They do so because they are made in God's image. If there were no ethical standards outside of ourselves, if we were truly amoral beings, then the existence of the idea of morality would be unexplainable. C. S. Lewis makes an excellent case for this point of view in his book *Miracles*.[1]

It is significant that religions the world over base their ethical norms on the will of their deities. They do not find the bases for decisions on right and wrong in their own actions or wills. But strangely enough the gods do not adhere to their own standards! Moreoever, because all religions of the world are polytheistic, with the exception of the Israelite religion and its three daughters—Judaism, Islam, and Christianity—there are

conflicting divine standards. Each god or goddess differs from
the others in his or her wishes. This confused situation means
that most world religions are not profoundly ethical in nature.
They give lip service to the idea of a divinely established ethic,
but they provide little practical guidance for their followers.
The reason for this shortcoming is obvious. If the gods themselves cannot agree on standards and do not adhere to the ones
they do agree on, what should their worshipers do?

Over against this stands the Bible. Biblical religion is profoundly ethical. The heart of the Old Testament, and thus of the
Bible, is the Torah, or "teaching." The Jews were excessively
proud of the Torah because they took it for what it is: the instruction manual for life, written by the Author of life. While
the rest of the world groped in darkness, wondering what man
was doing on this planet, they had the operator's manual.

The basis of the Torah is: there is one God; He is the Creator
of the world; His behavior is consistent with His character; the
creation is made to be consistent with His character; He offers a
covenant of grace and blessing to His creatures; He will bless
and care for them; and they, in turn, are to live lives that are
reflections of His character. So the statement is made, "You are
to be holy to me because I, the LORD, am holy" (Lev. 20:26).
*Holy* originally spoke only of "otherness," those qualities that
separated deities from humans. But the Israelites came to
realize that what set *Yahweh* off from them—and the other
gods—was His ethical character. Then they were astounded to
find that God intended to share that character with them!

Thus, the Ten Commandments, as the Old Testament represents them, are not the distilled wisdom of a primitive people
in a far-off place. As such, they would have only dubious relevance to our time. Rather, the commandments are presented as
being a distillation of the character of God. This being so, they
are essential not only to our right functioning but also to that of
the whole universe.

G. K. Chesterton says essentially this through his character
Father Brown. A thief had dressed himself as a cleric intending

to steal a priceless sapphire-studded cross that Father Brown was transporting. Certain that he had fooled the "simple" priest, the thief engaged Brown in a theological discussion. He asserted that truth as supported by reason is relative. To bolster his argument, he pointed at the first stars twinkling in the twilight sky and asked how standards that might be appropriate to this planet could have any relevance to the strange, unknown worlds out there.

Brown answered succinctly,

> Well, you can imagine any mad botany or geology you please. Think of forests of adamants with leaves of brilliants, think the moon is a blue moon, a single elephantine sapphire. But don't fancy that all that frantic astronomy would make the smallest difference to the reason and justice of conduct. On plains of opal, under cliffs cut out of pearl, you would still find a notice-board, "Thou shalt not steal!"[2]

## The Bible Is the Word of God

But is the Bible correct in its representation of itself? Is it really the Word of God? Has God given us His plan for life in its pages? Does the Bible reveal God's patterns of moral behavior? There are three answers given to these questions: yes; no; and yes, but. . . .

On the negative side, it is argued that the Bible is on exactly the same level as the holy books of other religions: the result of man's search for God. Thus, its pronouncements on ethics are no more binding than those of the Hindu Rig-Veda, for example.

The affirmative side holds that the Bible both records and is God's self-revelation in and through the historical experience of the Hebrew people.

The third alternative is the one heard most frequently today. I have called it the "yes, but" response. This view affirms that God has revealed Himself to humanity but denies that the Bible is itself the revelation of God. Rather, the Bible is a human witness to, and interpretation of, whatever means God has chosen by which to reveal Himself. This means that only the broadest, most general principles may be said to derive from God. Specific statements are attributed to men.

This present volume is written from the affirmative position. The writers believe that the Bible, as we have it today, has its ultimate source in God. To be sure, it has come through the hands and minds of persons in different cultural settings. This has lent variety to style and emphasis. But this has not altered the basic thrust and content of the material. The remarkable unity of scriptural teachings attests to this. It is as if some stunning gem were shown in several different settings; each setting would highlight different facets of the gem, but none would change what the gem itself was.

But what evidence supports the view that the Bible is itself the revelation of God's character and will and is thus prescriptive in matters of morals and ethics? The primary evidence lies in the distinctive world view of the Bible. When taken as a whole, that world view is startlingly unique.

To be sure, at many individual points there are similarities between the biblical world view and that of Israel's neighbors. But those similarities relate to superficial matters and not to essential ones. Now, if someone were to point out that both my dog and I have brown eyes and conclude therefore that either he is human or I am canine, would he be right? Despite the superficial similarity, there are some essential differences. In the same way, to point out that the Mesopotamian creation story has an order of events similar to those of the biblical creation account does not thereby demonstrate similarity in essence between the two. In fact, they are essentially different.

What are the essential features of the biblical world view? They are: God is one, transcendent, uncreated, asexual, personal. He cannot be represented at all, especially in any natural form. He cannot be manipulated, but He longs to bless people who will respond to Him in personal faith, trust, and obedience. He is utterly consistent and trustworthy. The system He created is good, but fallen. Humanity, male and female, is the highest and best of creation. The human problem is not insecurity, but alienation. There is a distinction between humanity and nature that must not be blurred. Existence is not cyclical, finding its meaning in recurrence; rather, it is linear, moving from promise to fulfillment, finding its meaning in the unique, nonrecurrent events that the Bible accurately records. Individual differences are significant and worthy of record. The body is good. Ethical behavior is rooted in the consciousness of God's behavior toward oneself. Thus love, honor, justice, and faithfulness are not simply desirable but obligations, because they describe the character of God. I could go on, but this is enough to convey the central features of the biblical teaching.

These features are unique to the Old Testament. Neither the Egyptians, the Mesopotamians, nor the Greeks—all infinitely more brilliant in metaphysics and philosophy than the Hebrews—have given us a total world view anything like this. So where did it come from? The most common answer is: The Hebrews had a certain genius for religion. But the Hebrews disclaim any such genius. They describe themselves as stubborn, stiff-necked, and hard-hearted. They report that they were dragged, kicking and screaming, into an understanding they did not want and that God laid hold of them and would not let them go even when they bit the hand that held them.

For these reasons, then—the Hebrews' own claim and the very inexplicability of the biblical world view apart from that claim—we assert that the Bible is indeed the Word of God. Because of this, we believe it has a demand on us and on our lives. Through the Bible God shows ways that are right and will lead to fulfillment and completion and ways that are wrong and will lead to emptiness and disintegration.

## The Bible Speaks to Every Moral Issue

It is in the confidence that the Bible is the Word of God that we approach it regarding any issue of life. In some cases, no specific word is given. This does not, however, permit us to disregard the Bible and do what we wish. Rather, it calls us to the difficult task of sorting out other evidence, drawing implications, and coming to a conclusion that will then provide the basis for our practice as faithful followers of the living God.

Such conclusions must always admit the possibility of contrary judgments. The matter of abortion is an example. The Bible speaks no specific word on this issue. But by the process just outlined many have come to the conviction that abortion is always wrong in God's sight. This may be so, but lacking a specific word from the Bible itself, we must allow the possibility of abortion being right in some circumstances.

The matter of adultery is different. It is evident from numerous clear statements in the Bible, and even more numerous allusions, that adultery is never right. On this issue there is simply no other answer for those who submit their ethical decisions to the authority of Scripture.

It is with regard to such clear ethical teaching that situation ethics has been so destructive. Through the use of bizarre experiences, such as the famous prison camp episode (in which a woman wonders whether she could justify having relations with a man on the grounds that she would be released if she became pregnant), it is suggested that the ethical norms that govern our daily lives are always up for renegotiation. Whatever the good intentions of the situationists may have been, the actual result of their teaching has been the dissolution of ethical standards in daily living as more and more persons have found "good" reasons—usually hedonistic and self-serving—for disobeying clear scriptural teaching.

But some may say, "The idea of absolute ethical standards is an Old Testament point of view. I submit to the authority of Scripture, but it is the authority of the New Testament. The only prescription in the New Testament is love. Whatever is the loving thing to do, that is right."

This is a distortion of the New Testament teaching. To be sure, the New Testament teaches that love is the highest and only adequate motive for action. But a false dichotomy has been set up by the popular situationists' rationale. It is suggested that the choice is between loveless standards and a loving lack of standards. That is not so. The choice the New Testament puts forth so forcefully is: obedience to God's standards for the right reason, i.e., love; or obedience for the wrong reason, i.e., self-righteousness. The New Testament does not abrogate the standards of the Old Testament by its teachings on love. Rather, it forever shuts the door on a person's patting himself on the back for a rigid observance of certain commands when his heart is empty and cold.

Jesus' teaching on adultery is an example of this. Far from loosening the Old Testament command, He strengthened it. Can a man congratulate himself for not being an adulterer just because he has not been in bed with a woman other than his wife? No! Unless his love for his wife, his love for that other woman, and his love for God is such that he does not need to mentally undress that woman, he does not know the meaning of obedience.

Jesus' statements to the man who is called the rich young ruler follow the same pattern (Matt. 19:16–21). He does not suggest that by following Him the young man can dispense with the commandments. Rather, Jesus calls him to add to his obedience a kind of commitment that will transform that obedience from something negative into something positive.

Paul's teachings are along the same lines. He logically attacks the idea that by external obedience to the commandments we can win God's favor, or having once received it, keep it (e.g., Gal. 3–4). He argues in the famous love chapter (1 Cor. 13) that love takes precedence over all other motives as the springboard for action. Does this mean all ethical norms are "up for grabs" in Paul's mind? Are they open to reinterpretation or even annulment? Can love declare something right today that was wrong yesterday? Hardly. What is often conveniently overlooked is that when Paul finishes detailing the folly of trying to please God through external obedience, he invariably reminds his readers that love will manifest itself through an ethic and a life style that are of the same fabric as that portrayed in the Old Testament (Rom. 4, 5, 8, 12, 13; 1 Cor. 5—10; Gal. 5; Col. 3).

The New Testament declares that external obedience out of a heart that is cold and proud is displeasing to God. But the Old Testament says the same thing in numerous places; for instance, Ezekiel wrote of a "heart of stone" (Ezek. 36:26). These classic words were used to summarize the whole Law: "Love the LORD your God with all your heart and with all your soul and with all your strength" (Deut. 6:5), and "Love your neighbor as yourself" (Lev. 19:18); but this understanding had gotten lost in the externals. The New Testament reiterates and reestablishes it in the light of the cross.

Thus, love does not release us from adherence to the ethical norms of the Bible. Rather, it calls us to a new and deeper obedience because of its own compelling power. "Christ's love compels us," Paul explains (2 Cor. 5:14).

In conclusion, then, the writers of this volume believe, with John Wesley, that the Bible constitutes the oracles of God. Therefore, it is the rule of life, not only for us as Christians, but for all the world. If this position is correct, then it is possible to discern God's attitude toward all of life, including our sexuality. The church diverges from that attitude only at the peril of losing its identity as the people of God.

## Two World Views: Pagan and Biblical

In order to understand correctly the Old Testament's attitude toward homosexual behavior, it is necessary to probe more deeply into its world view as contrasted with that of its neighbors. This is important because much of the biblical ethic is directly rooted in that world view. It is sometimes implied that the biblical teachings are a vast hodgepodge of materials, somehow thrown together. That is not true. Once it is understood how the Bible sees the world and what a radical departure that view is from the pagan world view, many teachings that seem quaint and unrelated suddenly take their places as integral parts of a system that has powerful claims on the lives of people today.

## The Pagan World View

First of all, let us look at the pagan world view. *Pagan* is used here, not in a pejorative sense, but only as a term synonymous with "nonbiblical." But this immediately raises the question, Which nonbiblical view? For there appear to be several. As a matter of fact, there is really only one nonbiblical world view. The details presented here are drawn largely from the ancient Near Eastern religions, including Greece and Rome, and extending from 3000 B.C. to A.D. 300. However, a study of other world religions shows the same underlying rationale in them as is found in the religions of the ancient Near East, as well as an unusual number of similar details. This is not to say that all nonbiblical religions hark back to the same source. Rather, they are fundamentally the same, because they all follow the same procedure for obtaining religious knowledge. They proceed from the given, the physical world, and create a picture of ultimate reality on that basis. Whoever follows such a procedure will find that the result will always be essentially the same.

A rather stunning example of this is found in the books of Carlos Castaneda, who describes his initiation into the thought and world view of an American Indian sorcerer in the 1960s. Although there are some unique details, the basic structure of thought is uncannily similar to that found in the ancient Near East five thousand years earlier.

The fundamental principle of the pagan world view is that of continuity. This is the idea that all things that exist are continuous with one another. There is no distinction between humanity and deity, deity and nature, nature and humanity. Dr. G. Herbert Livingston, my teacher and colleague, has diagrammed the concept of the basic identity of these realities as shown on page 26.

The circle contains all that is—the universe. It is a closed system with nothing beyond it. Nothing leaves it, and nothing penetrates it. Within this system the three compartments are functional only. There is no distinction among them as to their natures. They differ only in role. Thus, the gods are different from humans, but not really other than they. They are the same kinds of beings ethically, behaviorally, and substantially.

Another way of expressing this basic principle is by calling it the law of correspondence, that is, things that are alike are equal. This idol is like Baal; therefore, it is Baal. Thus, what is done to the idol is done to Baal. But follow this one step more. Baal is like the storm: he is potent; he is life-giving; he is impetuous; he is destructive. Therefore, he is the storm. Thus, what is done to the idol is done to Baal, and what is done to Baal is done to the storm. In this way the worshipers can force the storm, assuming no barriers have arisen among the three realms, to do their will. The purpose of pagan religion was to insure that human beings could shape divine and natural events to enhance their own security. For that function to be realized, it was essential to deny any boundaries among the three realms.

This process also worked in reverse. Not only did humans wish to make the gods do what the humans wished, they also wanted the human and natural realms to do what the gods did. This is exemplified in their means of maintaining order.

Perhaps the most deadly thing to human security is chaos. Societal organization, achieved with great difficulty, crumbles overnight. Material well-being, so necessary to the good life, can be wiped out in a moment by a flood, a storm, or an epidemic. How can one prevent such disorder, which always seems to be hovering in the wings?

The concept of continuity suggests that what takes place on earth is only a shadow of what is taking place continually in the heavenly realm. Thus, if chaos threatens here, it must be because it is actually threatening there on a continual basis. But since this earthly realm is orderly overall, it must mean that the gods are continually triumphing over the forces of chaos.

The problem is: How can we get the benefits of that continual victory for this particular annual cycle or this particular event? And perhaps even more importantly, how can we insure the continuation of the gods' victory on an ultimate level? Both of these can be accomplished by reenacting the story of the divine conquest of the chaos monster. Since the actors act like the deities and dress like them, they are continuous with them. This means that once more chaos is defeated, the gods' hands are strengthened, and the effects of the divine conquest are actualized for this specific year and situation.

Given the understanding that ultimate reality takes the same shape as this world and, indeed, is completely continuous with it, certain conclusions follow. These conclusions relate to the nature of deity, sexuality, time, space, persons, and ethics.

If deity is continuous with this world, it must be obvious that monotheism is impossible. There must be many gods, one for each force or element in the universe. Furthermore, since the gods are part of the system, they are conditioned by the system and can be manipulated through it. If one does something to the bull who is like Baal, he does something to Baal. Again, since the gods are continuous with both nature and humanity, they share all the characteristics of both realms. Although they are sometimes kindly and helpful, at least as often they are arbitrary, tyrannical, and selfish. Just as nature seems to be without ultimate purpose, so the gods have none. Like humans, they are basically interested only in self-aggrandizement. Thus, the gods are not to be trusted. The appropriate attitude toward them is wariness. Manipulate them if possible, fawn on them if necessary, but don't trust them.

Like all the rest of this world, the gods are fully sexed. This is quite understandable if ultimate reality is in the image of this world. Life on this planet exists because of sex. Thus, the gods exist because of sex, and, in turn, it is because of their sexual activities in the real realm—the divine—that life goes on here in this shadow realm. If one asks for the mystery of life and answers it in terms of this world, the answer is obviously sex.

Particularly is this true in an agricultural society where reproduction of plants and animals is the key to survival. If fields and flocks are infertile, people will starve. If either a husband or his wife are sterile so that the couple remains childless, their living has been pointless; the family line will disappear. Thus, sexual potency becomes all-important, and figures of fertility—the bull, the ram, and the pregnant or nursing mother—become central images of the divine.

How is the ideal fertility and potency of the divine transferred to the human and natural realms? Again, continuity is the key. On a national level, the king and a priestess would have intercourse. Because of their correspondence to the sky god and the earth goddess, that divine pair's continual copulation is actualized for this particular year and the seminal rain can be expected to fall into the womb of the earth and fertilize it. Of course, this same activity could also take place on a local level in response to more individualized needs.

What about events in time? What conclusions about the significance of such events can one draw from acceptance of the law of continuity? These events are significant only as they are continuous with other events. What is different is insignificant. Only what is the same has any meaning. For this reason, only the beginnings of things, which are being continually acted out in the divine, are important. Time has no goal, no sense of progress. The ideal is an endless cycle in which all things grow out of and, as nearly as possible, repeat the beginnings. Thus, the unique, the individual, events are unimportant. Precisely because they are discontinuous with previous events, they are not worthy of consideration. The pagan does not want to remember last year's large flood or the abnormally small rainfall of the year before. By remembering them, he might perpetuate them. What he wants to perpetuate is that ideal rainfall that will be just right because it will be exactly continuous with its heavenly counterpart.

The same is true of space. The significance of any space lies in its correspondence to divine space. Thus, in Egypt, the building of a symbolic hill inside a temple insured that this was the place of that primeval hill where creation began. And if the temple down the road also had such a hill in its precincts, then that too was the place. If you were to say, "But wait, it couldn't have happened in both places," the pagan would look at you very strangely. "But of course it did," he would respond. "Both hills are like the primeval hill. Therefore, both hills *are* the primeval hill." The idea that a place has its own importance because of its relationship to events in time and space is not consistent with the law of continuity.

The same is true of persons. Those unique characteristics that set one off from the masses are precisely the characteristics that do not matter. Discontinuity is insignificant. An individual is no more significant than a snowflake falling into the ocean. Humanity as an ideal is what matters. Persons matter only insofar as they are continuous with the ideal.

Finally, the law of continuity produces some very serious conclusions concerning ethics. Since there was no purpose in creation, there is nothing that can be said to be in keeping, or out of keeping, with that purpose. Furthermore, since nature knows nothing of right and wrong, but only of survival, then neither do the gods. Finally, since ethical behavior has nothing to do with receiving the blessing of the gods, but only imitative and manipulative behavior, ethics are hardly necessary to the good life. To be sure, proverbial wisdom as to how to get along with the least uproar in this kind of a world could be very useful, but the idea that some things are right whether anyone knows about it or not is all but unintelligible to those who operate on the principle of continuity.

What, then, is the heart of the pagan world view? It is the idea that the physical universe is all there is to reality and that all beings, forces, and events within the universe partake of one another. There are no distinctions between the various components, nor is there any purpose behind the existence of such components. The major value of human life is security. Such security is solely dependent on one's ability to control those persons, forces, and events that impinge on one. This control is achieved through the manipulation of power, either material or spiritual, that is inherent in the system.

Fundamental to this whole conception is the idea that there are no boundaries. There are no limits, no areas out of bounds. If there were boundaries, one could not lay hold of universal power. But when one begins to deny boundaries, the results follow quickly until it becomes plain that in such a universe everything is fated. Its destiny is predetermined through its continuity with other things. The pagan is locked into a cosmos without meaning, freedom, or dignity, and from this cosmos the only hope of escape is annihilation.

Does this pagan world view have any currency in the modern, scientific West? Surely the Westerner is too intelligent to fall for such superstition! Unfortunately, intelligence has nothing to do with it. The Egyptians, the Babylonians, and the Hindus were at least as intelligent as we, and maybe more so. This world view is the best that the unaided human mind can devise. Is it current in the modern Western world? Yes, it is everywhere. Consider the fundamentals. The universe contains everything that is. There is nothing outside of it. All existence is composed of the same basic stuff, and all combinations of that stuff are random, without purpose. People live for security, and power is the way to security. The most powerful, thus most secure, persons are those who know best how to manipulate their environment. They are people who know how to destroy boundaries, how to get in touch with the origins of things, how to lay hold of the sources of power. History becomes increasingly meaningless and unimportant as the now, with its immediate connections with power and security, becomes all-important.

Increasingly, we have become enamored of spiritual power. Interestingly enough, the road began with a denial that there was even a spiritual reality. Matter is everything, the philosophers of a century or two ago argued. Educate a man, a woman, as to the material realities, then turn them loose on the world, and they will solve our problems in short order and give us the security we crave. Knowledge—physical, antispiritual, secular knowledge—is power, they said. And we bought it. The world is ours, we said. There are no limits to what we can do with it. We do not say that so glibly anymore. We have discovered that the problems are too big. Where now shall we go for power?

We have turned, and are turning, to an old sexualized spiritism. We were not wrong in believing that this physical universe is all there is to reality, we say. It is just that there is a spiritual component that we had previously overlooked, that's all. This step toward spiritism is inexorable once the boundary between ourselves and God is denied. Either we will be made in God's image, or a god will be made in our image. If a god is made in our image, he is a terrible taskmaster. He leads us directly away from what had been thought to be the good, the beautiful, and the true to bind us to the opposite of all of these.

Having found the problems too large to handle with the resources at hand, we have gone in search of other resources. Have we turned to God, who expects commitment, fidelity, and responsibility? No. We have turned to spirit powers we believe we can control through imitative ritual. We turn inward to the exploitation and the exhibition of our own sexual power, convinced that somehow the mystery of identity lies there.

Thus, the old gods rise from the dead. Nor is education proof against this resurrection. The more educated a person is, the more susceptible he is, unless there is an undergirding of biblical faith. Spiritism is sweeping the intelligentsia of Brazil at an unprecedented rate. North America is but a step behind. We have chosen our world view and the results are upon us.

Astrology is a fascinating example of this revival of paganism. The worship of the "starry hosts" (Jer. 19:13) is older than civilization. (The present names of the constellations in the astrological calendar are simply Greek and Latin translations of the ancient Mesopotamian names.) Astrologists teach that, since we are continuous with the stars, their configuration at the moment of our origin shapes us. No commitment is required, no historical responsibility is demanded. Our lonely individuality is submerged; only our continuity with that ideal pattern matters. But if we admit any distinction, any boundary between ourselves and the stars, the whole structure falls to the ground. Suddenly we are finite, vulnerable, lonely, and responsible. That we do not want.

### The Biblical World View

The biblical world view stands in stark contradiction to the pagan view. In every significant particular the Bible differs from such an understanding of reality. Why does it do so? Because it has a different underlying principle. Instead of the law of continuity, the Bible organizes its world view around the law of transcendence. That concept can be diagrammed thus:

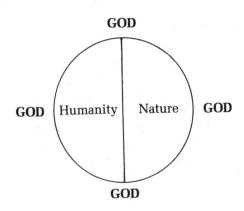

In direct defiance of the rest of world thought, the Bible conceives of a God who is not part of the universe. He is outside of it, apart from it. He everywhere penetrates His universe; He is not cut off from any part of it; but He is neither contained in it nor conditioned by it. He is radically discontinuous with the world. He transcends it.

This recognition that God is not conditioned by His creation opens the door for several positive affirmations. First of all, though the world consists of many parts, He is One. Second, though the world appears purposeless, He is purposeful. Third, though the world seems untrustworthy and inconsistent, He is fully trustworthy and consistent. He transcends creation in every way.

On the other hand, this understanding that there are clear distinctions between God and the world makes several demands. God cannot be represented by any created thing, for He is other than creation. One dare not attempt to control Him through the manipulation of creation, for He is not part of it. God is not just a superhuman, and His character ought not to be depicted as such. Sexuality cannot be attributed to God. It is a feature of the system, but not of Him. He may not be worshiped through sexually based rites. He, not sex, is the mystery of life. God is not continuous with nature. He may be seen in the storm or the sun, but He is neither. He transcends them. They only reflect His glory and power.

But this principle of transcendence has ramifications for the system as well. Just as God has made a boundary between Himself and creation, so He has built boundaries into creation. One of the major boundaries is between humanity and nature. Humanity transcends nature. Paganism attempts to assert human control of nature through the affirmation of continuity between humanity and nature. But the Bible recognizes that only as humanity is distinct from nature and receives authority over it from the Lord of nature can it ever become the master He intended it to be. To deny this is to dehumanize humanity and to destroy nature. Both humanity and nature are creatures of God, partakers of the same stuff, but distinct in essence and character. And since humanity transcends nature, humanity has a special significance and worth in the scheme of things.

Time also has significance in the light of the law of transcendence. The transcendent Creator has a purpose in creation that a mindless system producing itself could not have. Beginnings are significant, but not determinative, for the past can be transcended. Humanity is not doomed to repeat it. Thus, events since the beginnings have their own importance as they relate to the will of the Creator. Precisely those events that are discontinuous become significant and worthy of record because they are different from the past and may point the way toward the goal.

In the same way spaces have their own unique worth in relation to the unfolding of the Creator's purposes. There is no primeval drama, taking place outside of time and space, to devalue this time and place. The drama relates to what has taken place once for all in this time and space as unique persons have struggled and failed, or succeeded, in the will of the One who made them. Each place has its own significance. It does not rest in some mystical continuity with everything that has been.

What about that pile of rocks beside the Jordan? Is it of no significance in itself? Does it only partake of the significance of some a-temporal, a-spatial hill? No! That pile of rocks has an enduring significance because here a once-for-all, never-to-be-repeated event occurred: God's people entered the land and they intend to remember that (Josh. 4:1–9).

Thus, the irony of the two principles begins to emerge. Continuity, which says there is no boundary between us and God, takes reality out of this changing, developing realm and rests it in some mysterious unchanging one. On the other hand, transcendence, which sees a sharp distinction between creation and Creator, makes this present realm precisely real.

The same understanding relates to our importance as individual human beings. Exactly at the point where we differ is the point of our significance. Where we transcend the norm, where the boundaries can be drawn between us and other human beings, there is our true identity. When we stand alone, yet not alone, before Him whose transcendent purposes offer us real choices and genuine responsibilities, there we matter.

It is no accident that the idea of an individual's worth and dignity is almost the sole possession of the Western Christian tradition. Neither is it an accident that with the disappearance of that tradition from the West, awareness of individual worth and responsiblity is going with it.

Given this understanding of time, space, and humanity, it is no wonder that the Bible manifests a consciousness of the significance of history some seven hundred years before the Greek Herodotus, whom some call the father of written history. For what is history? It is an attempt to give some account of those persons, places, and events that are judged to have had a significant impact on subsequent events. Without the biblical world view, there are no significant persons, places, or events on this earth, nor is there any historical development.

Finally, the principle of transcendence has deep implications for our understanding of ethics. First of all, we cannot control God's blessing through manipulation of the environment or through imitative ritual. There is no mechanical way to get the use of God's power for our own benefit—although across the centuries many Christians have tried, and many still try. God is transcendent. He cannot be moved through the system.

Second, as transcendent Creator, God has a single standard of behavior, which is in keeping with His own character. This standard is neither relative nor temporal, for He is neither relative nor temporal. Those who are rightly related to Him have no option but to allow that character to be reproduced in them. If they refuse to do so, the relationship cannot be maintained.

We cannot force God to supply our needs, but He wants to supply them if we will let Him, says the Bible. How can we let Him? We can do so by relinquishing our foolish grip on our own security and entrusting it to Him and by living a life in keeping with His purposes and character.

Thus, the ethical pronouncements of the Scripture are part and parcel of this remarkable world view. We are to treat persons in certain ways because of who God is; we are to treat nature in certain ways because of who God is; we are to treat ourselves, including our sexuality, in certain ways because of who God is. There are carefully prescribed boundaries around our behavior because there are carefully prescribed boundaries built into reality, and our behavior is to model that reality. Deny God's transcendence and one must deny all other boundaries as well. But it also works in the other direction. Deny the ethical boundaries of the Bible, and the end result is the denial of transcendence as the principle of reality. The two go hand in hand. It is not possible to accept one set of boundaries and deny the other for very long.

This is why paganism hurls itself at ethical boundaries. They must not be allowed to stand! They are a contradiction to the basic principle of continuity. Thus, for example, in the Canaanite city of Byblos, every woman had to prostitute herself to a stranger for one day during the festival of Adonis (Baal) or else be shorn of her hair.[3] Why? Because there are no genuine boundaries surrounding the husband-wife relationship and those boundaries that might grow up must be systematically dismantled. Of course, as we have seen, in the name of freedom they were chaining themselves to the relentless wheel of continuity.

On the other hand, the Bible goes to great lengths to defend and strengthen those boundaries around the marriage relationship. Why? Because they are part and parcel of the boundaries between humanity and nature, Creator and creation, apart from which there is no freedom to become all that we may be in the transcendent God's providence.

In conclusion, why does the Bible impose certain limitations on human behavior? Because behavior without limits serves and models a world view that is directly antithetical to the truth. One need not keep an image nor be a cult prostitute to be living a life that denies transcendence. One needs only to live as though he were the sole arbiter of right and wrong in his life, as though there were nothing to prevent him from doing what he wanted. Those who do so are living according to the pagan world view.

## THE BIBLICAL VIEW OF SEXUALITY

The world view that sees all things as continuous must see sex and sexuality as being terribly significant to the existence of the universe. The chain of reasoning goes something like this: all life—at least all that can be observed—is sexually generated; sexual potency and fertility are that on which all observable life depends for its continuation; therefore, sex is essential to life on earth and so to life everywhere.

Against such a backdrop, sex is full of mystery and power. The sex act becomes an act of worship. Through it one can storm heaven and lay hold of the very springs of life. Thus, what one does and says with sex becomes a profound religious statement.

The Bible denies all of this. In a word, it demythologizes sex. Sex is not an attribute of the cosmos, it is an attribute of creation alone. Thus, one cannot use sex to get to God. Nor can one gain power over one's own life and future through sex. To be sure, sex is a powerful inner drive. Because of this and because of constant temptation to use it in ways God never intended, the Bible puts careful boundaries around the expression of sexuality.

### Sex Is a Created Entity

To appreciate the uniqueness of the biblical truth that God is not a sexual being, one must read the pagan mythologies from around the world. First of all, the myths say the gods got here just as the rest of us did—through sexual procreation. They were sexually generated out of chaos, and those first gods then generated others. But the Bible makes it plain that God was neither sexually generated, nor did He so generate any-thing else. He is not continuous with the created system. The language of sexuality simply is not applicable to Him.

This recognition is very important for the current sexist debate. While God's roles are commonly defined in male terms, His nature never is. His genitalia are never described; His couplings with consorts—divine, human, or animal—are never mentioned; He is never defined as sexually male. He is not a sexual being.

But if this is so, why are God's roles more often described in male terms? Ought we not, if it is true that God has no sex, to begin to describe Him also in female terms for the sake of balance? I think not. There are two reasons for this. One is practical, the other more theoretical. The practical reason is that around the world mother cults are almost exclusively fertility oriented. Motherhood and childbearing are all but synonymous. Thus, to call God "Our Mother in heaven," given our tendencies to make sex sacred anyway, opens real doors to the sexualizing of God. Obviously, many male deities also are associated with fertility cults, but by no means all. Apparently, maleness is not so completely tied to reproduction in the human mind as is femaleness. For this reason then, male terms are more practical to describe the transcendent God. They are less prone to become entangled with sexuality.

The theoretical concern relates to our freedom to rewrite biblical figures of speech. Obviously, everything said in human speech about the infinite God must use images. The most we can say is, "God is like—," or "God acts like—," all the time knowing that the One-Who-Is is as far beyond our little images as the sun is beyond a speck of dust. But does this recognition leave us free to replace the biblical figures with new ones as situations change? I think not. Figures of speech are not totally divorced from the realities they represent. Consider, for instance, a figure like "the Lamb of God." Of course Jesus was not a lamb; He only gave Himself sacrificially. Therefore, since we understand the reality behind the figure, we are free to create new figures that will more aptly convey the reality, aren't we? But suppose the reality is much more complex than we suspect? And suppose that figure is more intimately connected to the reality than we know? Then, if we remove or change the figure, we destroy a part of the Bible's richness and capacity to speak on a variety of levels about the truth. Thus, I wonder if the biblical figure of God as Father does not have a certain appropriate relationship to the reality that lies behind it—a relationship that will be lost if we begin to shuffle it about.

But let it be said that just as God encompasses all the best of manhood, so does He also encompass all the best of womanhood. He has a tenderness, a gentleness, a sensitivity, and a hardheaded practicality that are nowhere seen so clearly on earth as in woman. But the point is that as the Bible portrays God, He is neither male nor female. So when He comes to create life on the earth, He does not do it through sex or sexually based conflict. Sex is not at the heart of the universe.

However, many persons, heartily affirming this truth, immediately plunge off the other end of the continuum and act as if sex were not part of the created order either. The Bible never makes this mistake. It is straightforward and matter-of-fact about sex in creation even as it denies sex outside of creation.

At once in the first chapter of Genesis, the basic fact of human life is asserted—that we are sexual beings, male and female. Why are we this way? The question is answered in the next breath—in order to reproduce ourselves. The fundamental purpose of our sexuality, though by no means the only purpose, is reproduction. This first biblical statement about sex, occurring as it does in the first biblical statement about humanity, makes it abundantly clear that whatever understanding of sexuality we have, it cannot denounce the male/female function of child-rearing and parenting.

## Sex Is a Dynamic Gift for Our Enjoyment

The God-given drive to reproduce explains, in part, the great power of sex. Someone once said, "Imagine a society where a group of people sit in a darkened room watching a large draped salver being moved about in time with moodily rhythmic music. As each successive drape is removed, the tempo and tension heighten. Finally, just as the lights go out, the last veil is whipped away to reveal—a succulent piece of roast beef!"

The reason the story seems so ridiculous, of course, is that no one would think of handling the desire for food in such a way. Why not? How is it different from the sex drive? There are different kinds of psychic energy behind each of these desires. We eat to preserve ourselves. We copulate to preserve the race. God made us to reproduce, and that energy, if not directed in appropriate ways, will express itself in inappropriate ways.

But not only did God make us to reproduce, which assumes male and female, He also made us male and female for each other. The second chapter of Genesis spells this out. In a way that is simple enough for a five-year-old to grasp, but profound enough to engage the most mature scholar, the Scripture lays out the essence of our joint sexuality. The issue here is, of course, human loneliness. It is not good for a person to be alone, says the writer. And all of us can attest to that out of our own experiences. The question is, however, what is God's intention for the meeting of that loneliness? What does Adam need? Does he need companionship, friendship? Yes, but his needs are deeper than that. He needs someone to whom he can belong and to whom he can give himself physically.

Most significantly, Adam is involved in the search. So always God preserves our dignity and insures the depth of our understanding by letting us discover what He already fully knows. The animals are led before Adam. God gives him the opportunity to define the problem and discover the solution, if he can. What he discovers is that the male, by himself, is not complete. If he were, he could bask in that perfect communion with God that was his birthright and need no one else. If he were complete, he could commune with himself in the expression of his completeness, needing perhaps only a pet as something on which to lavish care and affection. But after all the animals have paraded past him, Adam knows what God knew—someone is missing.

The words *it is not good* in this context are important (Gen. 2:18). All through the first chapter of Genesis, the recurring refrain has been, "And God saw that it was good" (vv. 10, 12, 18, 25). These are the words of an artist. In his mind, he has envisioned something. Now he has transferred that onto paper or canvas or stone. If the outcome corresponds to the vision, his response is, "That's good." But if it does not correspond, what then? Exactly what God said about Adam's aloneness.

Adam's aloneness was not the way God had envisioned humanity. The male was not enough to complete the full concept of "man." He could not, by himself, be a full person. Someone else was needed so that he, together with that other person, could know what it means to be fully human. That full humanity could not be attained through the creation of another male. The Creator's vision of full humanity was of two sexually differentiated components, each of the same stuff, on a par, the same, yet different, finding their fulfillment in mutual surrender. Adam's ecstatic response to Eve's creation was, in effect, "This is me, yet, glory to God, it's not me." God made us for each other.[4]

This understanding of our sexuality—that it is not fundamental to the universe but that it is fundamental to human make-up—means several things. Above everything else, it means that, within the bounds of mutual male/female commitment, we are called to a frank enjoyment of our sexuality.

A part of this call to enjoyment comes out of the demythologizing mentioned earlier. Sex is not the key to existence. It is not the source of our ultimate meaning. In itself it can offer neither heaven nor hell. Insofar as we, like our pagan forebears, expect too much of sex, make it too mysterious and powerful, we are not free to enjoy the very real, but strictly limited pleasures it can afford. Sex is simply one more part of God's good creation—a significant part, to be sure, and a highly charged part, but not the be-all and end-all of human existence.

A glance through some bookstores today ought to convince us that we are expecting "other-worldly" results from sex. Those who pander to this neurosis are getting rich while confirming us in our belief that one "atomic orgasm" after another is our birthright. And furthermore, they suggest, our present partner's inability to give us this is all that stands between us and ultimate happiness.

The Bible says that a less-than-ideal sex experience is not the cause of our problems, and an ideal one will not solve our problems. Like every other relationship in creation, sex is dynamic, sometimes highly satisfying, sometimes frustrating. But if we will let it be that and not ask more of it than it can give, we will find it offers much.

The biblical injunction clearly declares that sex is a delightful gift intended to be enjoyed. Proverbs 5–7 contains the best statement of this from the male point of view. The passage encourages a man to delight in his wife's charms, to drink deeply from her as from a well. It also warns him that if he thinks the adventuress can give more lasting satisfaction, he is mistaken.

By the same token, the Song of Solomon (known to the Jews as the Song of Songs, or "best song of all"), which depicts a male's uninhibited delight in his partner, also depicts the female's delight in him. That delight is a long way from the caricatured Victorian lady passively allowing her husband to use her while she thinks of other, more pleasant things. Our sexuality is God's good gift to us, and the Bible calls us to stop using it manipulatively. Instead we are to relax and enjoy it.

The Bible does not portray sex as possessing some mysterious power. It is a part of creation and, as such, is strictly limited. Having said all this, however, it is necessary to add that there is a certain mystic sense to human sexuality, as the Bible sees it. The copulation of a woman and a man is of a different order than that of a cow and a bull. Genesis 2:24 gives us the first inkling of this when it says, "For this reason (the fact that a man and a woman are made for each other) a man will leave his father and mother and be united to his wife, and they will become one flesh."

The sex act culminates that process whereby two sexually different partners are melded together into one new personality. This is why Jesus draws on this same reference when He speaks so strongly against divorce in Mark 10:7. Divorce does violence to that one new person created through marriage and gives back two half-persons.

Now sex, in and of itself, cannot produce that melding of personalities the Bible talks about. Sex has no power in itself. A wife separated from her husband told me recently that whenever they got back together they had great sex experiences, but that didn't solve their problem. And so it cannot. Sex must be the symbol of something that has taken place and is taking place. This is a part of God's lovely plan for us, not only in the expression of our sexuality, but in general. He has made us so that what we do with our bodies demonstrates the expression of our spirits.

This is part of the reason for the biblical use of the word *know* to describe sexual relations. When I was a sophisticated teenager, I chuckled a bit at the biblical writers. Poor inhibited souls, I thought. They could not simply come out in the open and admit that people had sex. Instead, so I imagined, they had to use a euphemism like *know*, much as we say, "We had Rover put to sleep," rather than, "We had Rover killed." As I got older, I discovered the Bible said exactly what it meant. Persons are not intended to have sex like a pair of dogs or a brace of quail. For humans, the sex experience is designed to be the fulfillment of a process of knowing, a process of mutual mastery and mutual submission. Just as the male and female bodies are made for each other, so are the male and female spirits, each supporting and complementing the other. Thus, the enjoyment of sex, as it grows out of a good relationship, cements our knowledge of one another in ways that are ultimately beyond intellectualizing.

This further explains the unusual power of sex over us. Not only do we have a deep biological need to reproduce ourselves, a need that will express itself whether we understand it or not, but we also have deep emotional and spiritual needs for sex experience. Unfortunately, both of these needs have become twisted. Deep within us is the sense that sex was meant to be the climax of a process of coming home—coming home to ourselves and coming home to someone else. Here we can submit ourselves and give ourselves; here we can be submitted to and receive from; here in the knowledge of another, we can know ourselves. But all this has become warped.

## Sex Demands Commitment

Now there comes a supposed need to receive without committing oneself, to use without cherishing, or to know without being known. The tragedy of humanity is that we have believed we could be gods, choosing our own rights and wrongs. Now, far from home, on a dark road, we hear the siren song of sex singing, "Find yourself in me." Ah yes, but only after we have found ourselves in the admission of our finiteness and of His right, not ours, to define right and wrong. (Cf. Romans 1 for Paul's enunciation of the views presented in these two paragraphs.)

This mystical power of sexuality to somehow bring to fulfillment the reality of commitment and self-giving explains why the language of love and marriage provides some of the deepest metaphors for the relation of God to human beings. Where better can there be found imagery to express God's concern for us. He delights in us as a lover in the beloved. He finds us as ravishing as does a groom his bride. He longs for us to know Him, as He knows us. He has committed Himself to us as irrevocably as Hosea did to his wife even though she forsook him for prostitution.

Let it be said again—this is all metaphor, figure of speech, conveying a deeper truth. God is not actually male, nor is Israel or the church actually female. But the experiences of love and marriage provide the best vehicle for beginning to understand what His love is like.

This rootage of the sex experience in commitment and self-disclosure explains why adultery is the worst of all sexual sins in the biblical catalog. It is a denial of commitment, a breaking of faith, and an act of treachery (cf. Mal. 2:13–15). This is why the commandment singles out adultery for attention. This is not to say that the Bible has no concern for other types of sexual sin. Rather, it is saying that sex that abuses a faith commitment to one's mate is the epitome of what sex was *not* meant to be. In the same way the commandment against false witness does not excuse other types of lying. It says that the epitome of dishonesty is that which abuses the neighbor.

Adultery is wrong because sex was designed to be the expression of total, unconditional commitment and self-giving. Marriage, then, typifies a theological truth. God has made a covenant with us that He will not break. He is faithful; He can be depended on. Adultery suggests this is not so. It suggests one can repudiate one covenant and, at least tacitly, enter another one. And if a human can, then God can. Never! Faithfulness is at the heart of God's character. He was faithful even to the cost of His Son. And we may—no, must—model that character to the world through the metaphor of our sexuality.

The difference between this view of sex as theological statement and the pagan view lies in the connection between the human act and the divine reality. The pagan says, "Through this activity I can, on the one hand, make God do what I do, and on the other, I can tap into His potency." The Bible says, "The world will understand the unchanging character of God only as your life reflects what He is like."

So the Bible portrays sex as something limited to creation. It is given for the purposes of reproduction and for the achievement of human completion. Particularly in this latter function, it serves as a vehicle to teach the truths of submission, faithfulness, commitment, and experiential knowledge. As a part of God's plan of creation, it is very good. If we will let sex be what it was meant to be and not ask of it more than it can supply, it will be a source of delight and satisfaction.

## Sex Requires Boundaries

It is precisely because sex is conceived by the Bible to be such a good thing that such careful boundaries are built around it. Boundaries do not exist because something is bad, but because it is good. Screwtape, the senior devil in C. S. Lewis's *Screwtape Letters*, says it very well when he informs his underling that Satan has never yet created anything positively evil; he can only take what his Enemy has created good and pervert it. The greater potential for good something has, the more power it can have for evil.[5]

Sometimes Christians who call for a certain modesty in dress are charged with having a bad attitude toward the body. "If you would just accept your body as something good," the challengers say, "you wouldn't have all these hang-ups." This sounds very convincing, but a study of history proves it false. Perhaps the people who displayed the body most, and reveled most in that display, were the Greeks. They must have had a high appreciation for their bodies, right? Wrong! The Greeks believed the body was evil. It was a prison that held the spirit captive. The only hope of bliss was somehow to escape that body and return to union with the divine. They flaunted their bodies as a means of proving dominance over them and expressing contempt for them.

On the other hand, the Hebrews believed the body to be a positive good. It was a source of pleasure and delight. As a matter of fact, they could not conceive of life apart from the union of body and spirit. Thus, the Bible teaches that the abundant life of eternity will be a bodily life. Paul runs out of words in trying to distinguish between the present body and the resurrection body but he leaves no doubt that the body is a good and essential part of creation and always will be.

Because of this, God led the Hebrew people to put some careful boundaries on dress. Because the body is good, we cover it. Because it is God's gift to us, we do not treat it lightly or casually. And because it is a gift, it is not ours to display on our own terms as if it were some achievement of ours. Furthermore, a person's body is not only a gift from God to that person, it is also God's gift to that person's spouse, and it is to be held in trust also for the spouse (1 Cor. 7:4). Do not abuse the trust, God says.

In the same way, the Bible builds boundaries around the expressions of our sexuality. It has so great a power for good that abuse of it can lead to evil. But beyond that, there are boundaries built around it because it is wrong to try to take hold of universal or ultimate power through it. It is strictly within creation, and its legitimate uses are strictly limited.

All of this is, of course, against a pagan backdrop. As we saw in the earlier section, the denial of boundaries is fundamental to paganism. The whole world view of the pagans is based on that assertion. Denying any boundary between themselves and God, they hurl themselves at all other boundaries. The idea that they are limited to one sphere of action or influence is heresy.

In this light the pagans' attitude toward standards of sexual behavior becomes more comprehensible. In the thought of paganism, such boundaries were not permissible. Boundaries around the husband-wife relationship were not permitted, and ritual prostitution was expected. There were no boundaries around the parent-child relationship, thus incest; no boundaries between male and female, thus homosexuality; no boundaries between animal and human, thus bestiality. This is not to say that the above practices were everyday occurrences. Obviously, even their society could not endure that. But these kinds of practices were a regular part of the pagan expression of sexuality.

A part of the reason for this was the understanding that the way to establish one's dominance over sexual power was to flaunt one's sexuality. The more bizarre and promiscuous ways in which one practiced sex, the more one brought its mysterious power under one's own control. The gods were understood to practice the same approach as they too sought mastery of the sexual power inherent in the universe. Thus, the mythologies are replete with every kind of promiscuity and perversion, all performed by the deities with sensual abandon. Most important, this was a part of the cult, where sex was used as a means, not only of partaking in a boundaryless existence, but also as a means of insuring that such an existence would continue.

Thus, the sexual practices of the Canaanites and others were not simply a rather strange and accidental feature of their culture. These practices were a theological statement, an expression of an overarching world view that was through and through at odds with the biblical one.

For these reasons, when the Bible talks about the boundaries of sexual behavior, it consistently sets them against the practices of their neighbors. The Hebrews were called to a different understanding of existence and thus to different standards of behavior. Worship of the transcendent God must never involve sexual imagery or sexual activity understood to have manipulative effect on Him. Similarly, the expression of sexuality must be consistent with a world view that knows of a purposeful Creator who ordered life in certain ways and according to certain patterns. There is a distinction between humanity and nature, and sex must not be used to obliterate the distinction. There is a distinction between a married male and female and the rest of the world. Sex must not be used to blur that distinction. There is a distinction between a parent and a child. Sex must not be used to deny that distinction. Finally, sex must not be used in ways thought humiliating or potentially degrading. For instance, a woman may not be forced to have sex during her menstruation. This was sometimes done among pagans as a means of showing male domination and of degrading the whole sexual process. In other words, it is a form of what is today called "kinky" sex. One gets one's thrills from doing, and inducing one's partner to do, what is considered bizarre or somewhat debauched.

48

Some have argued, however, that the Israelites' rather strict sexual mores are simply those of a rural, provincial people. Urban people around the world, it is said, have broader sexual tolerance. Thus, the argument is that the biblical sexual standards are really only subcultural in nature.

The answer to this is threefold. First of all, the entire thesis up to this point has been that these two approaches to sexuality have nothing to do with subculture. Rather, they grow out of two radically different world views. Both views are entirely self-consistent, as are their practices, given their two quite different principles. If one believes in a transcendent Creator who has an upright, faithful character and that He has created the spiritual world to operate according to specific principles as He has the physical world, then specific standards of behavior follow as surely as two plus two equals four. On the other hand, denial of such standards cannot long coexist with the understanding of a transcendent Creator. One or the other must change. It is no accident that Dr. Norman Pittenger, whose exposition of process theology is shot through with the principle of continuity, has authored a book calling for Christians to see homosexual behavior as acceptable.[6]

The second answer to the suggestion that the biblical standards are only those of a rural subculture is this question: How long was Israel rural, anyway? The great prophets of the northern kingdom spoke to a culture that had been urban and cosmopolitan for five hundred years. They themselves grew up in that culture. Yet tolerance for the steady influx of Canaanite morals and manners is hardly a significant element in the preaching of the prophets. Their world view, not their culture, shaped their preaching.

Finally, the pagans themselves recognized that their practices were dangerous to society at large. Heterosexual marriage was a practical necessity for societal stability. Thus, homosexuality, though practiced somewhat widely in Egypt and Mesopotamia and more widely in Greece and Rome, was technically illegal in all those countries. Similarly, the best of the

Greek philosophers regarded the sexual practices of their temples as constituting a moral cesspool and the temples as places where morals were destroyed and subverted, rather than upheld. If these practices were simply the result of a greater tolerance in the society, why should the practices be considered destructive of the society? They were so regarded because there is a law written on the heart (Rom. 2:15). Juvenal, the Roman satirist, was hardly a country preacher in the fundamentalist tradition, but he recognized that what was taking place in his society was not an increasing tolerance for differing life styles, but simply moral rot.

The British historian J. D. Unwin made a study of eighty-eight different civilizations. He said,

> Every civilization is established and consolidated by observing a strict moral code, is maintained while this strict code is kept, and decays when sexual license is allowed. . . . Any human society is free to choose either to display great energy or to enjoy sexual freedom; the evidence is it cannot do both for more than one generation.[7]

To use our sexuality in ways that do not accord with the Creator's character and the nature and purpose of the world is to court disaster.

Before we leave this section on the boundaries that the Bible sets around the expression of sexuality, a final observation is needed. Notice where the bounds are set. They are established outside of heterosexual marriage. Within such marriage there is virtually complete freedom. On the statute books of some states, there remain laws that seek to regulate how often and in what positions a married couple may enjoy sex. The Bible will have no part of this. To be sure, it rules out of bounds those uses of sex that will enslave and destroy. But within the boundaries, there is freedom to trust, explore, and give. The Lawgiver is not some prurient little person who, in the words of the late Paul Little, scurries around looking for someone who is having fun so He can shout, "Now you cut that out!" He does not seek to regulate and inhibit every action. Rather, He is the benevolent

Father who delights in His children's enjoyment and only wants them to know where the dead-end roads lie.

## HOMOSEXUALITY AND OLD TESTAMENT LAW

We turn now to a study of the specific Old Testament teachings concerning homosexual behavior. We have taken the pains to set the stage because it is absolutely essential to understand the context in which these teachings stand. They are by no means isolated statements but, rather, are part of a total picture.

There are two explicit prohibitions of homosexual behavior in the Torah. These are found in the book of Leviticus at 18:22 and 20:13. With their immediate contexts, they read:

> Do not approach a woman to have sexual relations during the uncleanness of her monthly period. Do not have intercourse with your neighbor's wife and defile yourself with her. Do not give any of your children to be sacrificed to Molech, for you must not profane the name of your God. I am the LORD. Do not lie with a man as one lies with a woman; that is detestable. Do not have sexual relations with an animal and defile yourself with it. A woman must not present herself to an animal to have sexual relations with it; that is a perversion. Do not defile yourselves in any of these ways, because this is how the nations that I am going to drive out before you became defiled. Even the land was defiled; so I punished it for its sin, and the land vomited out its inhabitants (18:19–25).

> If a man sleeps with his daughter-in-law, both of them must be put to death. What they have done is a perversion; their blood will be on their own heads. If a man lies with a man as one lies with a woman, both of them have done what is detestable. They must be put to death; their blood will be on their own heads. If a man marries both a woman and her mother, it is wicked. Both he and they must be burned in the fire, so that no wickedness will be among you. If a man has sexual relations with an animal, he must be put to death, and you must kill the animal. If a woman approaches an animal to have sexual relations with it, kill both the woman and the animal. They must be put to death; their blood will

51

> be on their own heads. . . . Keep all my decrees and laws and
> follow them, so that the land where I am bringing you to live may
> not vomit you out. You must not live according to the customs of
> the nations I am going to drive out before you. Because they did all
> these things, I abhorred them (20:12–16, 22–23).

The context of these passages is very significant. Both of
them are dealing with the sexual practices of Israel's neigh-
bors-to-be. Homosexuality is not singled out. It is but one part
of a whole package. The prohibition of homosexual behavior is
not simply an isolated result of what is presently called
"homophobia," that is, an irrational fear of a practice we do not
understand. Rather, it is seen as one more manifestation of a
total approach to sexuality, an approach that denies any
boundaries in creation and uses sex as a vehicle to make that
statement. Homosexuals are not being singled out as an oppressed minority.

### Homosexuality: Behavior and Condition

It must be pointed out that these Scriptures forbid homosexual *behavior*. Neither here nor anywhere else in Scripture
are persons said to be "bad" because they feel an attraction to a
person of the same sex. This is a very significant aspect of the
biblical understanding of human nature. While we are not responsible for our predilections, we are responsible for what we
do with those predilections, for our behavior can transcend our
feelings. This point of view is in strong opposition to prevailing behavioral theory today, a theory that argues that we have
no real control over our behavior. We are programmed by our
heredity and environment to behave in certain ways, and we
will behave in those ways, like it or not.

Of course, the corollary of that position is the fact that we
are thus neither responsible nor accountable for our actions.
Thus, a homosexual person might rationalize: Who can say that
what I did was "wrong"? I didn't ask to be this way; so it's not
my fault. The people who programmed me this way probably
didn't know what they were doing either; so, it's not their fault.

It is nobody's fault, and if it's nobody's fault, it can't be wrong.

This point of view is an expression of the law of continuity. It says that I am continuous with the beginning influences that shaped me and am no more, and no less, than the sum of those influences. Furthermore, my actions and my feelings must be continuous. If I did not act out what I feel, I would be traitorous to the real me. I must be free to be me! This is a strange kind of freedom, this acquiescence to forces over which I supposedly have no control and for the results of which acquiescence I bear no responsibility. This is not humanization, but dehumanization.

The Bible stands in direct opposition to this point of view. It offers the possibility of transcending heredity and environment. Of course, heredity and environment influence us, but they do not determine us. We have a real choice whether to actualize the image of the transcendent Creator in us or to further deface that image. Surely this invests the word *human* with a grandeur and a dignity that is sadly lacking in the philosophies of today.

America was built on this biblical conviction. Simply because a person had a terrible background did not mean he or she was locked into it. Those who wanted to could transcend that background. Abraham Lincoln is one of the best examples.

So the Bible offers us the freedom not to act out our feelings. The story of Cain and Abel presents a beautiful example. Cain did not have to act out the anger he felt. It did not have to master him, as, for instance, Esau's anger did not master him. Thus, when Cain failed to exercise the mastery that was his, he was responsible for his action. But the initial feeling of anger was not the sin. The sin was in surrendering to that feeling.

We do not have to act out our desires, either mentally or physically. If we refrain, we are not to blame for having the desires any more than the alcoholic is to blame for having a desire for alcohol.

Some would suggest that the Bible's teachings are irrelevant precisely because they do not take account of homosexuality as a condition. It is argued that had the biblical writers known of such a condition they would not have spoken so strongly against the action out of the condition. But the premise is questionable, and the conclusion does not follow in any case.

First of all, there is every reason to believe that the biblical writers did know of homosexuality as a condition. Certainly the apostle Paul, whose prohibitions are as strong as any in Scripture, would have encountered this condition among the peoples of Greece and Ionia. Furthermore, the writers of the Old Testament also would have encountered it among the sophisticated inhabitants of Canaan. It is a fallacy to suppose that the people of the Old Testament were naive and parochial, living in a backward part of the world. The ancient Near East was highly sophisticated a thousand years before Abraham was born and it was to remain so for fifteen hundred years after he died. And Abraham's descendants lived squarely on the crossroads of the ancient world.

But even more importantly, why would the biblical writers judge the moral quality of the activity differently if it springs from a supposed condition rather than from the choice of someone looking for a new "kick"? If this is a wrong use of sexuality, it is wrong in either case. The subtle suggestion is that something is not wrong if "you can't help it." That brings us right back to our starting point. The ultimate moral quality of an act is not relative to our preconditioning. Rather, it relates to that act's congruency with the character of God and the resulting nature of creation.

## Homosexual Behavior and the Nature of the Law

But do these prohibitions have universal force? Is it not possible that they were valid, even revelatory, for that time and place but of no significance for today? For instance, the law specifically forbids the eating of pig meat, yet most Christians eat it today with no flicker of conscience. Why should we regard the prohibition of homosexual behavior any differently?

First of all, it is important to understand what the law is and what its function was and is. The historical context is crucial to such an understanding. The people had been delivered from Egypt through an act of God's grace. It was not through any moral rectitude or intellectual worth that they had been freed. Rather, it was simply as a result of God's choosing to shower His love on them. But why did He do so? He did so in order that they and the whole world might know Him. Over and over in the first twelve chapters of the book of Exodus, it is said that the purpose of the whole exercise was this: "You will know that I am the Lord your God" (6:7, et al.).

By the time of the Red Sea crossing, both the Egyptians and the Hebrews knew that they had not encountered some localized Midianite mountain god. This being was God. But beyond His overwhelming power, who was He? God's purpose of self-disclosure had only begun. How could He show the Hebrews, and through them the world, that He is not simply power, but, more importantly, integrity, faithfulness, consistency, and love, and that true godlikeness, or holiness, consists of these? He did so by entering into a binding agreement, or covenant, with the Hebrew people. The law functions as a part of the total covenant document. It describes what those who are in covenant with the Creator do. Thus, its primary purpose was instructive. The Jews indicate this in their title, *Torah*, which means teaching.

The covenant went something like this: "I agree to be your God. I commit Myself to you to care for you, defend you, and bless you. You agree to be My people. You must therefore live lives like Mine. You must...." Then follow the Ten Commandments, which are a short form of the stipulations of the covenant. The rest of the law is a fleshing out of the meaning and implications of the commandments. Its purpose is to teach what God and His world are like. The Torah was never intended to be a means of justifying sinners before God. That idea was a much later perversion.

The fleshing out of the law is recorded in the remainder of Exodus, Leviticus, parts of Numbers, and all of Deuteronomy. It includes three kinds of materials: instructions concerning civil life, instructions concerning religious ceremony and worship, and instructions concerning moral life. The latter give us direct moral teaching as found, for example, in the Ten Commandments. Those in the former categories teach moral principles through certain kinds of behavior. These kinds of behavior may no longer be relevant, but the principles still are.

This function of the civil and ceremonial law can be illustrated in this way. In the civil area some statements are made concerning responsibility. The particular behavior in this illustration relates to a vicious bull (Exod. 21:28–32). If one had such a bull but did not know he was vicious and he killed someone, the owner would be responsible, but in a limited way. On the other hand, if the owner knew the bull was vicious and he killed someone, the owner must bear full responsibility. Well, I have no bulls; so, this instruction says nothing to me. Right? Wrong. There is a principle of responsibility in God's universe. Suppose the brakes fail on my car and I crash into someone and maim or kill him. In any case I bear a certain responsibility, but if there had been no prior indication of impending brake failure, that responsibility is limited. On the other hand, if it can be shown that I knew full well those brakes were bad, then the whole blame and responsibility are mine. In summary, the specific behavior described in the civil law may deal with that era only, but the teaching applies to all times.

The interpretation of the ceremonial law is similar. Considerable space is given, for instance, to the delineation of clean and unclean foods. Some have argued that certain foods are intrinsically unhealthy and were forbidden to the Hebrews for that reason. Pork as a harborer of trichinosis is, of course, well known. However, when we understand the Torah's purpose as being to teach the character of God, a deeper function of the ceremonial law emerges. This is to teach spiritual truth through object lessons.

It is important to remember that the Hebrews were spiritual infants when they came out of Egypt. They knew next to nothing about spiritual realities except by intuition, and that, if we accept their own testimony, was none too sharp. How does one go about teaching abstract truth to infants? Concrete things may be used to demonstrate intangible principles. God very definitely had some principles to demonstrate. He is not continuous with the world, particularly the world as it has become. Thus, it is possible for one to have attitudes and behaviors that contaminate and defile with respect to God's character and nature. Other thoughts and actions may leave one spotlessly clean, spiritually speaking, because they are consonant with His nature.

Now how can such highly abstract truths be conveyed? Well, one might very well use foods, which a person will handle every day of his or her life, as an object lesson. If people ask themselves at every meal, three meals a day, for a thousand years, "Will this food leave me clean or defile me?" one might expect that by the end of that time they would have gotten the point that there is a difference between clean and unclean. Then they would be ready to learn that defilement is not a matter of food but a result of certain attitudes. The individual is contaminated from the inside out and not vice versa. This is, of course, exactly what Jesus said (Mark 7:14–23).

Virtually the entire ceremonial law functions as an object lesson to teach abstract spiritual truth. The sacrificial system is another example. Can the blood of bulls and goats take away sin? Are people continuous with those dying animals? Of course not, and the Bible is very careful to guard against having sacrifice understood in those ways (cf. Ps. 51:15–19; Isa. 1:10–20; Mic. 6:6–8). Unless there is faith and repentance and obedience, the sacrifice avails nothing.

But, at the same time, how does one get people to recognize that sin must be punished, that it is a matter of life and death, not simple mistake, and that forgiveness is never possible without atonement? How does one prepare persons to recognize God's provision for sin? The death of an innocent, perfect animal, perhaps the future sire or dam of one's flock, in place of oneself, the guilty criminal, became a powerful symbol of the theology of sin and forgiveness.

Because of the nature of the ceremonial law as object lesson, its function was distinctly temporary. When the reality had come, as it did in Christ, the symbol was no longer necessary. This is not to say, however, that the truths it taught were temporary. The defiling and contaminating power of sin is real; it is only that dietary laws are no longer needed, or should no longer be needed, to teach that point. By the same token, there is still no forgiveness of sin without the shedding of blood, but in the light of the cross, we should hardly need the death of animals to understand that truth.

The entire law is teaching certain principles about the nature of God and His world. The ceremonial and civil parts teach those principles through requirements that are temporary. The civil law speaks to specific behaviors in that society, many of which are no longer practiced, and the ceremonial law calls for symbolic behaviors whose symbolism is no longer necessary.

However, in the third part of the law, the behaviors called for or prohibited are neither symbolic nor limited to a certain time and place. These teachings have been called the moral law. In these the behavior and the principle are synonymous, and they are for all people in all time. There are no qualifiers and no conditions. These are simply what those who are rightly related to God will do. The summary of the Torah, the Ten Commandments, is stated in such terms. The fact that the law is summarized as moral law helps us to recognize what has been affirmed above, that is, in and through all of its time-conditioned phrasings, the law exists to teach the moral character of God.

However, the Ten Commandments are only a summary of the moral law. They do not themselves constitute the entirety of the moral law in the Torah. The question then becomes one of distinguishing this kind of law from the other kinds. The distinction is not nearly so difficult to draw as some suggest today. In fact, in most cases it is quite clear.

The civil law, in particular, is relatively easy to sort out. It commonly deals with specific cases of civil life such as the goring bull already mentioned, the borrowing of another's tools (Exod. 22:10–13), or regulations concerning slavery (Deut. 15:12–18).

Likewise, the ceremonial law is relatively easy to recognize. If the instruction regards the form and use of ceremonies or ceremonial structures, its import is obvious. Also, such laws define actions or events that render one unclean for ceremonial purposes, such as the handling of the dead, having any hemorrhage or emission from the body, eating unclean food, and so forth. Each of these prevents one from taking part in the ceremonies for a stated time but has no other penalty.

There are other actions, however, that do not have to do with the just functioning of society or with the maintenance of the ceremonies. They are commonly stated in categorical imperatives, and the punishment, when prescribed, is death. They are thus viewed as offenses against God or against life itself. Such, for example, is the cursing of one's mother or father (Lev. 20:9) or the offering of sacrifice to an idol (17:1–9). These offenses are not related to either civil or ceremonial behavior. They do not render one unclean or require the payment of a fine. Rather, they are related to the basic functioning and ordering of life. The doing of these is wrong at any time in any place. To suggest that these actions, which carry the death penalty, are of no greater significance than the eating of pork, which only renders one ceremonially unclean, betrays a serious misunderstanding of the structure and context of the biblical statements.

The prohibitions of homosexual behavior are stated as moral law. Such behavior is categorically prohibited and the death penalty is prescribed. There are no relative conditions. To be sure, the commands are part and parcel of a comprehensive sexual ethic that is drawn up in direct contrast to the pagan practices. However, the rationale behind that ethic is not simply reaction to a life style that happens not to be Hebrew. In other words, these commands are not given just so Israel's national identity will be distinct from that of its neighbors. Rather, these activities are prohibited because they grow out of and lead to a world view that is radically opposed to that of the Bible. Adultery, incest, homosexuality, and bestiality are not prohibited because they are the incidental practices of Israel's pagan neighbors. They are prohibited because they deny the creation order of God and thus the very nature of God Himself. As such, they are not distinct activities that happen to be grouped together. Rather, they represent one common outlook on sex and the world, that is, the denial of boundaries. This is not to say that someone who engages in one of these practices will necessarily engage in the others. It is only to say that the philosophy behind adultery, incest, homosexuality, and bestiality is the same. It is a philosophy that denies transcendence with its teachings of firm boundaries between God and His creation and between various parts of that creation.

Some have argued, however, that there is a clearly time-bound command in this sexual ethic. That is the one prohibiting intercourse during menstruation. Surely, it is argued, this action has no abiding moral significance. It must have been merely subcultural in nature, perhaps growing out of a superstitious dread of blood. So, it is concluded, since this prohibition can be dismissed as being only subcultural, any of the others can be dismissed as well.

Apart from the somewhat dubious logic involved in such a procedure, further study shows that there is a moral significance to the prohibition. This commandment refers to the pagan practice attacking the woman and humiliating her even though, as a priestess, she might volunteer. It refers to a deliberate degrading of sex and one's sexual partner. This is a matter of morality and not mere convention. Furthermore, the assignment of the death penalty makes it clear that something more than simple sexual custom is involved (Lev 20:18). The commandment is speaking of a way of using sex, and it is perfectly in keeping with the basic import of the other commands. There is a view of sexuality that makes it an instrument for denying the basic distinctions of creation and a vehicle for asserting one's own dominance over creation. Such a view and its attendant practices are forbidden.

However, some have argued that the location of this material in chapters 17—26 of Leviticus, the so-called holiness code, invalidates it as moral law. The background to such an argument is this: For about one hundred years many Old Testament scholars have believed that the legal portions of the Old Testament date, in their present form, to 400 B.C. or later. This would place these portions about one thousand years after Moses. Particularly the book of Leviticus was felt to be late, an expression of priestly religion after the Exile. The emphasis on sacrifice, ceremonial cleanliness, and so forth, is pointed to as support for such a view. Chapters 17—26, which are unified by the repetition of the motivation clause in the directive "Be holy because I, the LORD your God, am holy," is seen as the heart of this priestly teaching, because it is asserted that the concern for holiness is a distinctly priestly concern.

Thus, it is argued, the prohibitions of homosexual behavior are the work of priests who come very lately onto the scene and are opposed to the practice merely because Canaanite priests engage in it rather than because it is false to the Hebrew moral order.

However, this conclusion does not follow. Even if one grants that the Leviticus content was late priestly material—a position it is by no means necessary to take—that does not prove its opposition to be on merely religious grounds. If the material is late, it still shows a remarkable unity with the rest of the Old Testament where the practices characteristic of paganism are attacked for their world view, not simply because they are non-Israelite. But furthermore, whatever the date of Leviticus and whoever were its transmitters, all the types of legislation discussed above—ceremonial, civil, and moral— are to be found in its pages. The prohibition of homosexual behavior is for neither ceremonial nor civil reasons. Nor does the location of the prohibitions in the holiness code in any way determine what kind of legislation it is. That can be understood only through direct study of each commandment and its immediate connections. As we have shown, homosexual behavior is seen to be a moral offense.

The implication of this argument is even more serious than the stated conclusion. That implication is that Leviticus, and indeed the entire law, has no divine authority. The law was not, they claim, received and transmitted through an inspired Moses. Rather, it is the work of the religious establishment, a group notoriously biased in its judgments. Surely our judgments are at least as valid as theirs, it is said, and probably more so. Reasoning this way, on what basis can we say that any of the Scripture is authoritative? The unique world view that the books of the Bible, despite diversity of style and content, hold in common argues for what the Bible claims—divine origin. If the Bible does mislead as to its origin, the whole talk of a biblical ethic becomes simply antiquarian.

A further objection to the universal nature of the Torah's prohibition of homosexual practice grows out of the observation that while both males and females are enjoined from intercourse with animals, only male homosexuality is specifically prohibited. Lesbianism is not mentioned. From this observation it has been concluded that the commandment against homosexuality is primarily concerned with the degradation of a male. In other words, it is suggested that the Bible is opposed to male homosexuality because it drags a male down to the level of a female. The commandment, then, is the work of a male-sexist society that does not care so much whether intercourse between members of the same sex takes place, but cares very deeply whether a male is treated like a female. Therefore, since we are now Christians and do not regard treating a male like a female as being degrading, homosexual behavior among males is permissible, as it always has been among females.

This novel interpretation rests on two very weak bases. First, it is an argument from silence: since the Bible is silent about lesbianism, lesbianism is permissible. But there are a number of other, more likely, explanations for this silence. For instance, opportunities for lesbian encounters were limited in the ancient Near Eastern societies where a woman's movement outside the home was somewhat restricted. Also, there may have been little need for a command relating especially to women because women in the ancient world expected to find their life's fulfillment in the bearing and raising of children. Given that fact, lesbianism may have seemed a disenhancement of a woman's selfhood and thus not desirable. The absence of lesbian behavior in the temples probably supports this hypothesis. On the other hand, impregnation by an animal could be distinctly desirable as a supposed way of overcoming barrenness, especially if the beast were understood to be continuous with a deity. Other alternatives could be offered, but these are enough to demonstrate that the Bible's failure to mention lesbianism specifically is hardly proof that lesbianism was permissible.

The second weak basis of this argument is the assumption that the Old Testament has the same misogynous views as those attributed to the rabbis in Jesus' time. Whether that attribution is entirely correct or not is open to question. But even if it could be shown that the rabbis had an even lower opinion of woman than it now appears, this would say very little about the Old Testament position. Rabbinical Judaism is not identical with Old Testament teachings. Jesus demonstrated this when He distinguished between the Pharisaic understanding of righteousness and the actual Old Testament position. The same is true regarding women.

The ancient pagan world exalted the female principle to the heights but trampled actual women in the mud. By contrast, the Old Testament treats women with remarkable respect and dignity. To be sure, the Old Testament position is not as fully developed as that of the New. For instance, in the Old Testament a woman could be treated as having less economic worth than a man. But, over all, she is given equal personal worth. In fact, many of the laws that feminists regard as sexist are precisely those that guaranteed the rights and the dignity of a woman in those cultural circumstances (for instance, her right to refrain from intercourse during menstruation and her right to demand that her brother-in-law fulfill his conjugal obligations in place of her dead husband).

In conclusion, there is no reason to imagine that homosexuality is forbidden for sexist, cultural, or religious reasons. There is every reason to understand that it is forbidden on moral grounds. However, the final argument for the universal nature of any Old Testament teaching is the New Testament. Whatever the New Testament, as the fullest revelation of God's will, disavows is no longer required. But whatever the New Testament picks up and reinforces is doubly required. As the second chapter of this book clearly indicates, the New Testament does restate the Old Testament teachings concerning sexual behavior.

Important for our thinking here is the qualification that the apostles put on the release of the Gentiles from certain portions of the law in Acts 15. Idolatry, eating of blood (an important pagan expression of continuity—drink the bull's blood and gain his potency), and unchastity continue to be forbidden. Obviously, the apostles are speaking of those complexes of behavior that are inimical to the biblical world view. In this context, then, unchastity relates to all sorts of sexual license, as spelled out in Leviticus 18 and 20.

## Male Cult Prostitution

Among the practices forbidden to the Israelites was the employment of male and female cult prostitutes (Deut. 23:17). The technical term for these was *dedicated ones.* That is, their lives had been dedicated to the respective gods and goddesses so that their human sexual capacities might be used to serve the gods and the pagan understanding of the world.

The Authorized Version translates *dedicated one* as "sodomite" wherever this term refers to males (1 Kings 14:24; 15:12;

22:46; 2 Kings 23:7). Thus, it has been customary to see the strongly negative view of the Old Testament toward male cult prostitution as one more indication of the wrongness of homosexual behavior.

One objection to such a position has been that those who practice homosexuality today are not doing so for religious purposes. Thus, it is said, the Bible's attitude toward cult prostitution says nothing one way or the other about homosexual behavior today. This objection has been answered already by showing that the connection between the pagan world view and homosexual practice was not a casual one, but a direct, causal one. Because their world view denied the possibility of boundaries, the pagans practiced homosexual behavior. For whatever reason the activity is practiced, it expresses a world view that is profoundly religious.

However, the argument has recently been taken one step farther. Derrick Bailey, in his influential book *Homosexuality in the Western Christian Tradition*,[8] denied that male cult prostitutes were homosexuals! In that the Hebrew word, as noted above, has no etymological connection with sodomy, there are some grounds for such a statement. On the other hand, where did the English translation get its basis for its unequivocal translation? That basis extends back for about fifteen hundred years through every preceding version and translation to Jerome's Latin Vulgate, which was completed about A.D. 400. In that version the Latin word for homosexual appears in all the references. Why was this word used? Surely it was because in Rome homosexuality was one of the official functions of the male cult prostitute. This would have been no less so in Canaan.

The version of the Old Testament in wide usage before the Vulgate was the Greek Septuagint. Normally the Septuagint translates the Hebrew rather literally. In these cases, it translates the term as "male prostitute" three times, gives the Hebrew word in Greek letters once, and in the fifth occurrence translates it "one who changed his nature." Although only the last specifically supports the rendering of the Vulgate, the others certainly do not contradict it.

Bailey's chief reason for denying a homosexual function to the male cult prostitute is that it does not make sense for a fertility cult to employ homosexual activity when fecundity is desired. This stems from a fundamental failure to understand paganism's refusal to admit distinctions. Any sexual activity would produce the desired divine result if the ritual were performed correctly. Furthermore, it is highly likely in a sophisticated society like that of Canaan that there were a significant number of males who would have a preference for male sexual companions. Yet these men also would want to manipulate the deities' powers of fecundity. The temples would be obligated to provide ritual prostitutes for such.[9] Thus, while the Hebrew word does not technically mean sodomite, there is every reason to believe that the functions of male cult prostitutes involved homosexual practices.

## Homosexual Behavior an Abomination

The strong feeling of the biblical writers against homosexual behavior stems from their understanding that it is an "abomination." (The word occurs in both Leviticus 18:22 and 20:13 in the Authorized Version.) But what is the meaning of "abomination"? Does it simply mean disgusting, as in English, or does it have deeper connotations?

There are two Hebrew words that are regularly translated "abomination." They are *shiqquts* and *to'evah*. *Shiqquts* occurs thirty-seven times and seems to have special reference to idols and unclean food. Ten of its occurrences are in Leviticus 11, where it refers to eating amphibians, reptiles, water animals without fins or scales, birds of prey and carrion eaters, winged creeping things, and creeping vermin. On two other occasions the word also refers to food (Isa. 66:17; Zech. 9:7). The association of these with carrion and filth probably explains the strong terminology.

The remainder of the occurrences of *shiqquts* all refer to

idols, where the term is used as a synonym for idol with mocking intent. Thus, for instance, 1 Kings 11:5-7 does not call Chemosh and Molech the idols, or gods, of Moab and Ammon respectively. Rather, the writer calls them the "abomination" of Moab and the "abomination" of Ammon (see also Deut. 29:17; 2 Kings 23:13; Jer. 7:30, et al.). The well-known abomination of desolation in Daniel is an instance of this (9:27; 11:31; 12:11). Instead of saying that Antiochus Epiphanes would erect a statue of the Lord of the Heavens, Baal Shamayim, Daniel says that the *shiqquts shomem* will appear. He has substituted *shiqquts* for the divine name Baal and *shomem*, or "desolation," for *shamayim*, "heaven."

To'evah occurs much more frequently (125 times) and has a wider range of meaning. It is the word used of homosexual behavior in particular and of the whole catalog of pagan sexual behavior in general (Lev. 18:26–31). Kenneth Grayston well sums up the central connotation when he says abomination refers to "anything repugnant to the true nature of person or thing."[10] To be sure, there are instances where this repugnance is culturally rooted, as in Genesis 43:32, where eating with Semites is said to be an abomination to the Egyptians. But, by and large, the references are to matters much more deeply rooted in the biblical perception of the world.

Given the fact of a transcendent Creator, whose character is not simply a reflection of this world, it becomes possible to say that there are some things that are in keeping with His plan and character and other things that are not. Pagan religions cannot say that. Their only data for making ethical decisions come from this world with all its relativities and ambiguities. But God, the true God, is outside of this world. Thus, He is able to say, "It is repulsive to Me to see you doing things I never intended."

This concept is best seen in the dozen or so occurrences of *to'evah* in the book of Proverbs. For instance, false weights and measures are said to be an abomination (11:1; 20:10, 23). Why? Because they are a denial of the single standard of creation—a certain volume of a given metal will weigh the same tomorrow as it did today. For it to do otherwise, or to use a lighter weight as if it were a heavier, is an abomination to a consistent Creator. Likewise, it is abominable to twist justice (17:15). There is one standard by which all are judged, the character of God. Thus, it is abominable for a king, who is expected to establish justice, to do evil (16:12).

But perhaps the greatest denial of the creation order is the denial of God Himself (Ps. 14:1; 53:1). This explains why idolatry and its attendant practices are abominable (Deut. 18:9; 2 Kings 16:3; Ezek. 18:12, et al.). They are not an abomination because they are non-Israelite; they are an abomination because they are false to the world as God made it. They grow out of a wrong world view and they lead inevitably to a distortion of everything true.

"Abomination," then, does not merely define something thought to be done by pagans. Rather, paganism is abhorrent because it involves abominations—attitudes and practices that are false to the creation order. Idolatry is false to creation because it makes God in man's image and suggests we can manipulate God without reference to our own ethics. Adultery is false to creation because it is falseness embodied, that is, it is to be false to the one who has given himself or herself to that person. Homosexuality is false because it denies the distinction between male and female. Bestiality is false because it denies the distinction between human and animal. In itself, each of these practices is a falsification. They were incorporated into pagan worship because they served its purposes. If they are separated from such worship, they do not suddenly become true. Paganism did not make them false to God's creation, and removal from paganism cannot make them true to it.

In summary, the Torah clearly and explicitly condemns homosexual practice. It condemns it because it serves to express a world view antithetical to that of Scripture. As a result, homosexual behavior came to be a part of that false view of sexuality that was a focal part of pagan religion and worship.

There is no reason to conclude that the prohibition of such behavior is any more time-conditioned than are those of adultery and incest. Like them, it does not relate to ceremonial uncleanness or civil justice. It is a moral offense, indicated in part by its carrying the penalty of death. Unlike adultery and incest, however, homosexuality is singled out in its prohibition as an abomination. This indicates that the writers saw it as an especially significant denial of the creation order.

### HOMOSEXUAL BEHAVIOR AND THE BOOK OF GENESIS

In the previous section, I referred continually to the creation order. Although I have already dealt with this in regard to the biblical view of sexuality, it will be good to recapitulate those statements with special reference to homosexual behavior before going on to refer to the Sodom and Gomorrah incident.

As I have maintained throughout this discussion, the biblical understanding that this world is the creation by fiat of a single, transcendent, self-consistent Being has far-reaching implications. The idea of a single ethical standard in keeping with that Being's own nature and with His purposes in creation is not only possible but likely. If we then accept the Bible's claim that through it, and through it supremely, God reveals Himself, we have in it His statement of what we were made for and how we should live.

### *The Significance of the Creation of Male and Female*

In this light it becomes plain that homosexual behavior is contrary to all that God intended in creation. When Genesis makes its first statement about humanity, it immediately says that humanity is composed of male and female elements (1:27). In other words, both are essential, the one to the other, for real humanity to exist. But some might argue that this is simply a broad descriptive statement indicating that there are males and females in the world with no necessary demand that they cohabit for true humanity to be realized. The Bible answers that by stating that they are male and female that they might reproduce (v. 28). In other words, He made them for each other, that together they should multiply. Since multiplication is obviously the result of cohabiting, this provides the ruling interpretation for the continuation of the statement. As together they multiplied, then together, as a cohabiting pair, they are to bring the earth under control and care for it. Humanity is intended to be male and female functioning in intimate partnership.

The second chapter of Genesis only furthers this understanding. Another male would not be the fulfillment of Adam that God envisioned. The whole point of Genesis 2:18–25 is that for human personality to find fulfillment it had to be separated into male and female components, which components could then find union in the self-giving of two sexually differentiated persons. Thus it is that "unisex"—the idea of blurring or eliminating distinctions between the sexes—is an abomination to God. The statement in Deuteronomy 22:5 that forbids a person to wear the clothing of the other sex has sometimes been used to argue that women should not wear pants. The absurd nature of such an appeal (in that men were not wearing pants when the commandment was made!) has often obscured the real point. That point is that one should not dress (in whatever style) so as to deny one's sex. It is thus speaking to the "drag queen" and the transvestite and not to evolving styles in clothing. The use of the term "abomination" (AV) gives us the clue here. The command concerns something false to the creation order.

Let me say a word about those who say homosexual behavior is not wrong for them because it is not contrary to their nature. But is nature a genetic trait or a pattern of learned behavior? Granting the fact that this is their "nature," does this change the moral order of creation? Does the fact that some persons are alcoholics "by nature" change the Bible's teachings about drunkenness for those persons? Will they find their true "selves" by gratifying their "nature"? No. Right and wrong are not determined by proceeding from humanity to God. (That is what the Fall in Genesis 3 was all about.) Right and wrong are determined on the basis of the character of God and His purposes in creation. It is then that He offers us the possibility of transcending our natures—who, for instance, does not have a fallen nature?—and of behaving in keeping with His nature and the original plan.

## Sodom and Gomorrah

The other passage in Genesis that has relevance to our discussion is found in chapter 19. It is, of course, the story of Sodom and Gomorrah. It is only recently that any question has been raised about the implications of that account. The church's understanding of it has been uniform for nineteen hundred years. So much has this been so that the word *sodomy* is a fixed part of the English language as a euphemism for homosexual behavior.

Apparently, the first voice to issue a clear call for the reinterpretation of Genesis 19 was that of Derrick Bailey in 1954.[11] However, numerous others have followed him since that time. Bailey seems to be of the opinion that this story constitutes the main basis from the Old Testament for prohibiting homosexual behavior and that if the account has been wrongly understood, any rationale for condemning the activity disappears. However, as shown above, whatever the Sodom and Gomorrah account may say, the teaching of the Torah stands on its own and offers a quite sufficient rationale in and of itself.

Even so, Bailey's argument that there was no homosexual behavior referred to in Genesis 19 is insupportable. Marvin Pope gives the argument a very sympathetic hearing and then concludes succinctly,

> Whatever the influence of Jewish reaction to the homosexual practices encountered in the Diaspora, there can be no question that the understanding of the Pseudepigraphists and the church Fathers was well-founded, that the Sodomites' offense, like that of the men of Gibeah (Jgs. 19:22), was the demand for carnal knowledge of a neighbor's guests."[12]

71

Briefly, Bailey argues as follows: the homosexual interpretation of the sin of Sodom is forced on the passage. Neither the Old Testament, nor the Apocrypha, nor the Talmud treat it in this way. Only the pseudepigraphists, the Jewish writers Philo and Josephus, and the supposedly questionable New Testament books of 2 Peter and Jude do so. Nor do the clear biblical prohibitions of homosexual behavior appeal to the Sodom and Gomorrah (or Gibeah) story for support. This added to the fact that the accounts themselves do not call for such an interpretation would seem to make the argument conclusive.

However, there are a number of weaknesses in Bailey's argument. Let us start with the stories themselves. They are:

> But before they lay down, the men of the city, the men of Sodom, both young and old, all the people to the last man, surrounded the house; and they called to Lot, "Where are the men who came to you tonight? Bring them out to us, that we may know them." Lot went out of the door to the men, shut the door after him, and said, "I beg you, my brothers, do not act so wickedly. Behold, I have two daughters who have not known man; let me bring them out to you, and do to them as you please; only do nothing to these men, for they have come under the shelter of my roof." But they said, "Stand back!" And they said, "This fellow came to sojourn, and he would play the judge! Now we will deal worse with you than with them." Then they pressed hard against the man Lot, and drew near to break the door (Gen. 19:4–9 RSV).

> As they were making their hearts merry, behold, the men of the city, base fellows, beset the house round about, beating on the door; and they said to the old man, the master of the house, "Bring out the man who came into your house, that we may know him." And the man, the master of the house, went out to them and said to them, "No, my brethren, do not act so wickedly; seeing that this man has come into my house, do not do this vile thing. Behold, here are my virgin daughter and his concubine; let me bring them out now. Ravish them and do with them what seems good to you; but against this man do not do so vile a thing." But the men would not listen to him. So the man seized his concubine, and put her out to them; and they knew her, and abused her all night until the

morning. And as the dawn began to break, they let her go (Judg. 19:22–25 RSV).

Biblical commentators have always understood that *know* here has sexual reference, as it does in Genesis 4:1, for example, and several other places. However, Bailey points out that the word *know* has sexual reference only 14 times out of a total of 943 occurrences. Therefore, he suggests, the odds are against its having a sexual reference here. This interpretation is astonishing. Odds have nothing to do with linguistic usage. Context determines meaning. If the word never had a sexual usage elsewhere, but the etymology permitted it and the context demanded it, that would be enough.

What about the context? First of all, notice that both passages use the word *know* with unmistakable sexual connotations. Genesis 19:8 speaks of "daughters who have not known a man," and Judges 19:25 says, "They knew her, and abused her all night." The context is clearly sexual and suggests strongly that when the inhabitants demanded to know the visitors, they were speaking in sexual terms. If they were merely proposing to get better acquainted with the travelers, as Bailey suggests, the offering of the daughters and the concubine makes no sense. Bailey turns this latter point around and argues that the women would have been abhorrent to the men if they had been "truly" homosexual. The Bible does not say they were "truly" homosexual, whatever that is. It implies from the abusing of the concubine in Judges 19 that they were, in one of today's terms, "kinky." It is simply that for those men sex with males was a little more bizarre and, therefore, desirable. That the intentions were sexual is supported by the fact that both accounts agree that such action would be wicked (Gen. 19:7) or vile (Judg. 19:24). Nor can the deep hostility of the men toward Lot for refusing their demand be, as Bailey suggests, merely pique at Lot's accusing them of inhospitality (an accusation it is hard to see in the text). In short, both contexts suggest very strongly that homosexual "knowledge" is the subject.

But, Bailey says, the references to Sodom and Gomorrah in

the rest of the Old Testament do not indicate that they were destroyed because their inhabitants were homosexual. Neither does Genesis. God had made up His mind to destroy the cities before the homosexual outrage (Gen. 18:20). Why? Because they had gone the full route described in Romans 1. That road begins with pride and leads to idolatry and adultery and homosexuality. In other words, it was a culture gone totally false. To say that it was destroyed because it entertained homosexuality is like saying a dog was destroyed because it bit a child. In fact, the dog was destroyed because it had rabies. The biting was only a symptom.

## Second Peter and Jude on Sodom and Gomorrah

The evidence of 2 Peter and Jude that homosexuality was a significant symptom of the condition cannot be denied quite as easily as Bailey denies it. He says that these references are the result of late Jewish interpretation and thus are not a reliable indication of the original interpretation. It is curious that Bailey accords so much weight to this original interpretation, when he doubts that the event took place at all. If the event never occurred, neither interpretation makes any difference. On the other hand, if the event did occur, as there is every reason to believe, and if the Bible does record a divine interpretation of the events of human history, then that interpretation is of great importance.

The idea that original interpretations are better than later ones has grown up with the idea that the Bible is not a unity. Thus, those interpretations that are close to the event are likely to be more valid than those that are distant from it. This, of course, denies that the Bible could be written from a single, divine perspective as God inspired different writers. Instead, the Bible is seen to result from a number of differing theologies and viewpoints being superimposed on each other. The interpreter must strip off the often-contradictory overlays to get at the original truth that set the particular concept in motion.

Whatever one may think of this idea of the Bible's growth,

Professor Brevard Childs has pointed out quite correctly that the canon in its present form is that to which the church submits for its authority. To say that one submits to the supposedly early but not to the supposedly later, or vice versa, is a repudiation of all that the church was saying in canonizing this material. What was the church saying? It was saying that this is the overall interpretation that is accepted as authoritative. Thus, Jude's statement that Sodom and Gomorrah engaged in "unnatural lust" (v. 7) is the church's final and most authoritative interpretation. And of course if one believes, as the writers of this book do, that the Bible, while showing considerable variety, is still a unity that depicts not only the church's self-understanding but, more importantly, God's self-revelation, then Bailey's attempt to divide off the statements of 2 Peter and Jude from the original interpretation becomes all the more unsupportable.

As I have tried to demonstrate, there is no division between the Old and New Testaments over the interpretation of the destruction of Sodom and Gomorrah. The cities were not destroyed solely because of the homosexual practices committed in them and in the absence of any other sins. The homosexual behavior was only a symptom of a deeper malaise. But saying that it was a symptom in no way reduces its seriousness or its real significance in the accounts.

### CONCLUSION

In conclusion, then, what is the biblical position on homosexual activity? It is prohibited to all persons of whatever psychological state because it is seen as a falsification of the created order of God. To condone it is to condone an entire world view that is at variance with the truth. Performance of such activity is incompatible with the biblical message that calls us to be conformed to the character of the transcendent God and offers grace whereby such conformance may be possible.

This biblical position is wholly relevant to our situation today. It offers us the freedom to transcend our environment and our heredity and become the persons we were designed by God to be. It offers us the dignity and meaning that genuine responsibility for our actions brings. It makes us persons and not automatons whose actions and feelings are predetermined by a meaningless melange of factors; persons, not organisms whose mindless acquiescence in that melange at any time and place some would call freedom. Such acquiescence is not freedom, but bondage. It does not bring us nearer to our humanity but drives us farther from it.

The Bible teaches that a Person has created this universe along the lines of His own nature and has given us the real choice whether to actualize His image in us or further deface it. Surely this invests the word *human* with a grandeur and a dignity that is conspicuously absent in the philosophies of today.

Yet it is to such philosophies that our culture is turning—turning from the biblical world view to the nonbiblical world view. As Christians, we have an opportunity to challenge that turning. Or, in our eagerness to be relevant, we may rush headlong to join our culture in what Malcolm Muggeridge, the British journalist, calls its "Gadarene plunge." All too many church leaders and members in our day are choosing the latter course. In defense of their choice, they claim that the biblical statements are too much bound to ancient times to provide any clear rule of faith and practice for today. This is not so. The timeless principles emerge from their historic context with stark clarity when the Bible is regarded as the embodiment of God's enduring truth.

This being so, our options are plain. We may accept the Bible's authority over us or we may deny that authority. If we choose the latter, let us say so. Let us say the Bible does not speak to our age and be done with it. Or, believing the Bible, let us be done with the high-sounding statements that allude to the necessity of advanced training in hermeneutics if one is to understand the "true" import of the text. Even the unenlightened understand that such claims simply deny the plain teaching of the text. The biblical position is clear. It is neither outmoded nor unworkable. Let us accede to it or deny it. But let us not betray it by bending the Bible to support the whims of the pagan culture that surrounds us.[13]

# 2

# The New Testament and Homosexuality

The author is a missionary of OMS International with specific service in the Greek New Testament. He holds the following degrees: A.B., Asbury College, Wilmore, Kentucky; B.D., Asbury Theological Seminary, Wilmore, Kentucky; M.A., University of Kentucky; Ph.D., Harvard University. Dr. Greenlee is the author of several books, including The Gospel Text of Cyril of Jerusalem, Concise Exegetical Grammar of New Testament Greek, and Introduction to New Testament Textual Criticism. He has had published in popular and scholarly periodicals one hundred articles dealing principally with the Greek New Testament. He has written articles for the Zondervan Pictorial Encyclopedia of the Bible, The Expositor's Bible Commentary, and other works.

## By J. Harold Greenlee

# Homosexuality
in the Old Testament
**in the New Testament**
in church history
in the physical and emotional
in the courtroom
in the church

**2** The New Testament is neither puritanical, prudish, nor ascetic in its attitudes and teachings. The New Testament recognizes sex, sexual conduct, and sexual distinctions. There is a saying that describes the Old West as the place "where men were men, and women were glad of it!" That point of view can be taken to an extreme, of course, in which sex receives undue and even illicit attention. Within proper limits, however, this quip reflects an attitude toward sex that is consistent with the New Testament—a recognition that men and women are distinct, that there is an attraction between them, and that they need each other. The New Testament is not Victorian either in its view of sex or its discussion of it. In the original Greek text it is even less so than in many English translations.

At the same time, the New Testament does not glorify sex nor give it the disproportionate prominence that many aspects of our Western culture insist on doing today. The New Testament treats sex as one important part of life, but not as the most important.

The New Testament view is that sexual desire is God-given and that it is divinely intended to issue, under proper circumstances, in sexual relations. These proper circumstances for sexual relations are specifically defined: within marriage, between husband and wife, and under no other circumstances. No person can read the New Testament in its original language or in the common translations of it with objectivity and come to any other conclusion.

### GOD CREATED THEM MALE AND FEMALE

There are two basic premises in the New Testament's treatment of sex. The first is that God "made them male and female"—two sexes, no more and no less (Mark 10:6).

Let us examine this New Testament premise in some detail. Not long ago such a detailed examination would have seemed to be belaboring the obvious and belittling the intelligence of the reader. However, the claims of those who are attempting to defend homosexual practices make it legitimate, and indeed necessary, to devote some space to this premise.

It is maintained by some that Jesus did not condemn homosexual practices. The other side of the coin is that Jesus never said anything in favor of homosexuality or indicated any acceptance or approval of it. The burden of proof rests with those who claim that Jesus, in complete opposition to the mores of His Jewish culture, could have approved of homosexual practices. Let us therefore see what Jesus says concerning marriage and sexuality.

In Matthew 19:4 Jesus says, "Haven't you read . . . that at the beginning the Creator 'made them male and female' . . . ?" This verse clearly implies that there are two forms of human life, and two only. The emphatic terms *male* and *female* (*arsēn* and *thēlys*) are used here rather than simply *man* and *woman* (*anēr* and *gynē*). This and the nature of the expression imply exclusiveness of categories, that is, these two and no other forms.

Jesus then quotes Genesis 2:24 as further support of this idea of male-female exclusiveness: "For this reason a man will leave his father and mother and be united to his wife, and the two shall become one flesh. . . . So they are no longer two, but one" (Matt. 19:5–6).

Why is there no mention of possible same-sex unions here? Jesus could have stated, had He wished to do so, that the principle of a husband becoming joined to his wife applied also to two persons of the same sex in a sexual union. Jesus felt free to modify the current interpretation by the Jews of some points of the Old Testament in words such as "You have heard. . . but I tell you. . ." (Matt. 5:21-22). Moreover, Jesus loved everyone. If, therefore, some persons are "born" homosexuals and their homosexual behavior is thus a valid life style, Jesus at this point might have referred to homosexuals and indicated His acceptance of their natural condition and needs. He could well have added some statement such as, "And I say to you that when a man becomes joined to any other man, or a woman to another woman, they likewise become one flesh." If Jesus accepted the validity of homosexuality, somewhere in the Gospels He ought to have indicated His disagreement with the Old Testament's condemnation of homosexual behavior as in Leviticus 20:13.

The plain fact is that neither here nor anywhere else in the Gospels does Jesus give the slightest basis for assuming that He considered homosexual unions, must less promiscuous homosexual behavior, to be an acceptable life style. Nor may we suppose that He was ignorant of homosexuality. Even if we overlook the Old Testament references, homosexuality was well known in the world of Jesus' day, although it was far less common among the Jews than among the Greeks and Romans.

Jesus does, indeed, recognize one possible alternative to marriage, that is, celibacy—whether voluntary or because of sterility at birth or by emasculation (Matt. 19:11–12). The only reasonable conclusion to draw from the Gospels is that Jesus considered the sole legitimate type of sexual relationship to be between one man and one woman in a permanent union.

This is not to say that homosexuals were not included in Jesus' circle of love. Jesus was no religious legalist, and some of His harshest condemnations were for those who were. He flatly told a group of Jewish priests and religious leaders, "I tell you the truth, the tax collectors and the prostitutes are entering the kingdom of God ahead of you" (Matt. 21:31). The story of the woman taken in adultery likewise shows Jesus' love for a person who was guilty of sexual sin (John 7:53—8:11).[1] Yet in neither of these instances is there any hint that Jesus' love for the person includes acceptance of, or condoning of, the sexual sin. To the woman taken in adultery He said, "Go now and leave your life of sin" (8:11).

## New Testament Concepts of Love

At this point it may be well to give attention to the New Testament concept of love, since some of the defenders of homosexual behavior maintain that love is their guiding principle. On the television program the *Today* show, for example, in mid-1977 a psychologist-minister who is a practicing homosexual stated that he was not concerned about the interpretation of the Old Testament story of Lot and the Sodomites. He said that he simply follows Christ's command, "Love your neighbor as yourself."

There are four principal Greek words for love. One of these is *eros*, which is the love between husband and wife and includes sexual love. This is a God-given and proper love. The word *eros* does not occur in the New Testament, although Paul recognizes and approves the principle of it. For example, he exhorts in 1 Corinthians 7:5, "Do not deprive each other except by mutual consent and for a time, so that you may devote yourselves to prayer. Then come together again so that Satan will not tempt you because of your lack of self-control." Here is a frank acceptance of sexual love in marriage and a rather clear implication that Paul did not believe that marital sex was to be limited to the specific intention of begetting children.

*Storgē* denotes natural affection between parents and children that is based simply on the fact of that family relationship. It evokes a response such as "I love him because he is my son" or "because he is my father." This word occurs in the New Testament in the negative form, in which the absence of this kind of love between parents and children is strongly condemned (Rom. 1:31; 2 Tim. 3:3). It also occurs combined with the word for "friend" (Rom. 12:10).

*Philia* is love between friends. This kind of love is mentioned frequently in the New Testament. For example, James says, "Don't you know that friendship with the world is hatred toward God?" (James 4:4). It was said of Jesus at the tomb of Lazarus, "See how he loved him!" (John 11:36). Again, Jesus called His disciples "my friends" (Luke 12:4).

By far the most common word for love in the New Testament, however, is *agapē*. God loves the world with *agapē* love (John 3:16), and we are commanded to love God, our neighbor, ourselves, and even our enemies in the same way (Matt. 22:37, 39; 5:44). *Agapē* is not an emotional love, but rather a recognition of the infinite value of a person. This love is to be given, not because of any personal qualities or virtues nor yet in spite of any defects or negative qualities, but solely because each person is a human being, an immortal soul created in the image of God, destined to live for all eternity, and, in God's sight, of infinite value. *Agapē* love implies acceptance of a person simply because he is a person—and this is the basis on which God accepts him and declares that he is valuable.

However, there is much confusion concerning this kind of love, as if this acceptance of the person were the end of the matter. It is not. God does accept each of us as a person, without regard to our virtues or faults. He accepts us, however, with the full intention of changing us from what we are to what we ought to be. Hebrews expresses it like this: "The Lord disciplines those he loves. . . . Endure hardship as discipline; God is treating you as sons. . . . God disciplines us for our good, that we may share in his holiness" (12:6–10). Paul says, "He chose us in him before the creation of the world to be holy and blameless in his sight" (Eph. 1:4).

Contrast this aim of biblical *agapē* with the statement of a United Methodist minister, John V. Moore, who speaks of relating himself to homosexuals: "Understanding God as the Word who came and dwelt among foolish and fragile mortals, I could not be intimidated to refrain from relating with people who were different from myself. I was enabled to receive in a new way God's treasures which always come to us in earthen vessels."[2]

Here is no seeking of the best interest of the person, in this case the homosexual, but merely acceptance and nothing more. This type of acceptance is not biblical *agapē*. *Agapē* love values a person as a human being, and for that very reason it is not content that the person should remain less than the best he can be by the grace of God. It therefore seeks to help the person find deliverance from all that is hurtful or inferior and to develop toward his very best. *Agapē* love accepts the alcoholic, the proud, the sexually immoral, the person filled with hatred or overwhelmed with an inferiority complex; but any attitude that is content to leave these persons in such conditions is not the *agapē* love with which God loves all men and with which He calls us to love all men.

Moore further illustrates the shallowness of his understanding of this issue by raising the question of the difficulty of a homosexual person's changing his behavior. He says,

> As I reflected upon the demand that those who are homosexual change their orientation, I wondered how I might respond to a similar demand. For more than twenty years, Barbara and I had gone to bed every night in the same four-poster. For a judge or a preacher or counselor to demand that I change my sexual identification struck me as absurd. For the police and my fellow citizens to put me in jail or deprive me of my job, I could regard only as unjust and cruel.[3]

Moore's inference concerning homosexuals' being deprived of employment is dealt with elsewhere in this book. We will here deal with only one aspect of his remarks.

Moore's comment ignores the question as to whether homosexual behavior is or is not in violation of the Scriptures. He attempts to equate the propriety of insisting that a person cease illegitimate sexual behavior with insisting that a person cease a perfectly legitimate type of sexual behavior. This is like saying, "I cannot insist that one man should stop robbing banks to earn his living because I would not want someone to insist that I stop operating my grocery store to earn my living"!

Now if, as some maintain, homosexual behavior is acceptable to God, then there is no conflict here. In this case the homosexual person can, with God's approval and a clear conscience, continue in his homosexual behavior. We will deal with this question later. At present, however, we are discussing the claim that God accepts a person even though he is a homosexual—a claim that implies that God is willing for him to continue in his homosexual behavior. This claim overlooks the fact that God's acceptance of a person has nothing to do with either that person's virtues or his vices. It also ignores the fact that God accepts us with the full intention of *not* leaving us as He finds us but of making us like Himself, causing us to partake of quality of holiness that is His own central characteristic.

## SEX, A GIFT OF GOD FOR SPECIFIC CIRCUMSTANCES

There is a second and related basic premise in the New Testament's attitude concerning sex. This is that sexual relations are God's will for a husband and wife, and for these exclusively, to be carried out solely within marriage. They are an expression of love and unity between husband and wife and the means of preserving the family and of propagating the race. Implied in this premise is the idea that the mutual enjoyment of pleasure that normally is, and always ought to be, a part of sexual relations is not their only purpose, but that sexual relations are also normally intended to accomplish the purpose of childbearing.

If it is true that sexual relations are exclusively for a husband and his wife, then all sexual acts outside of marriage are condemned. This condemnation is in fact as clear as one could ask in the New Testament. All homosexual acts fail to fulfill the purposes for which sex was created. The New Testament teaching about homosexuality is in sharp contrast with statements such as those of Troy Perry: "I believe that there can be loving experiences, even in a one-night stand. I truly believe that two individuals can meet and share their complete beings with each other, totally sexually too, and never see each other again; and remember it as a beautiful, loving situation."[4]

If such promiscuous one-night stands of homosexual activity would have God's approval, then surely He would approve of similar heterosexual encounters. But these God condemns as fornication and adultery! How then can we presume to claim God's approval of such an encounter in a homosexual relationship? If there is no room in Jesus' teaching for some type of a permanent homosexual union analogous to marriage, then it is sheer desperation to try to claim His approval of a homosexual action apart from any such union.

Advocates of homosexual behavior as a legitimate life style overlook one logical prerequisite: the legitimacy of extramarital and promiscuous heterosexual behavior. The logic of this is that fornication and adultery are, after all, only one step removed from what is proper by New Testament standards. That is, they consist of a type of sexual act that is legitimate but under circumstances that are not legitimate. Homosexual behavior, on the other hand, is two steps away from what is proper: not only does it involve illegitimate circumstances, but it also involves sexual acts that in themselves are perverted and grotesque.

It cannot be denied that homosexual behavior is commonly casual and promiscuous. Only infrequently does it consist of anything like a permanent relationship. This is too often overlooked in discussions of the subject. The Christian standard demands that there be no sexual relations prior to or outside of marriage. It is rare to find a homosexual couple in a settled relationship who had no sexual relations with anyone before or after establishing their union. Nor do the defenders of homosexual behavior argue to legitimize only settled relationships. They do not reject promiscuous homosexual behavior. Instead, they argue for their right to casual relationships. What they insist on is complete freedom for any type of same-sex acts and behavior, without restraint.

### HUSBAND AND WIFE IN THE NEW TESTAMENT EPISTLES

Now let us examine some other New Testament passages that deal with sexual relationships and marriage, to see what bearing they may have on the question of homosexuality.

#### 1 Corinthians 7:1-2

First Corinthians 7:1 states, "It is good for a man not to marry." Paul is here stating that celibacy is a legitimate option for those who feel led in this direction. He continues, however, by stating that the safer course is marriage: "But since there is so much immorality, each man should have his own wife, and each woman her own husband" (v. 2).

It is worth nothing that the Greek word *anēr* used in 1 Corinthians 7:2 means both "man" and "husband," and the Greek word *gynē* means both "woman" and "wife." Thus, in this and similar passages the language leaves no room for a same-sex union; such a relationship would have to be expressed in other words. For instance, the word *anthrōpos*, the more common word for "man," is a generic word that can also mean "person" without emphasis on gender.

The language of 1 Corinthians 7:2 implies exclusiveness. It is impossible to find in Paul's words here any room for other types of relationships than that of husband and wife. This passage cannot mean, "Let each man have his own wife or male bed-companion (*koinolektros*) and each woman have her own husband or female bed-companion." In these verses Paul recognizes celibacy as a legitimate life style and then recommends marriage (male-female) as a safer course. Why does he not admit the additional option of a homosexual union? Such relations were well known and practiced in Corinth and they probably could more readily have been made respectable in the Christian community of Corinth than in many other localities. If mere avoidance of sexual promiscuity was Paul's concern, a settled homosexual union would have served that purpose as well as heterosexual marriage. It is clear, then, that Paul did not consider a homosexual union a legitimate option for a Christian. There is no sufficient reason for his failing to include such an option in a passage such as this if he had considered same-sex unions proper.

In my references to Paul I do not imply that Paul's words are not authoritative Scripture uniquely inspired by the Holy Spirit. I present what Paul says in these passages as expressing God's inspired Word. This point is worth making, since some advocates of free homosexual behavior treat the apostle's opinions on homosexuality as being subject to correction. John V. Moore states, "I am still persuaded that Paul condemned homosexual acts. I disagree with his understanding of them simply as perverse choices. . . . His judgments did not absolve me from taking seriously the findings of contemporary researchers, nor my own experience."[5] Moore's conclusion is clearly that the judgments of Scripture may be amended by the conclusions of present-day authorities.

It is true that Paul sometimes speaks to a local situation; and when he does so, his conclusions or directions may or may not apply to our own culture and situation. But even in these passages his words were written under the inspiration of the Holy Spirit. In the passages under consideration here I find no factors that would rule out his words from general application.

Someone may question this conclusion in view of some of Paul's comments in 1 Corinthians 7. In verse 12 he says, "To the rest I say this (I, not the Lord). . . ." But here his meaning is that he does not have a specific word from Jesus' earthly ministry to which he can refer the Corinthians, as he did in verse 10: "I give this command (not I, but the Lord). . . ." In verses 25–26 he states, "Now about virgins: I have no command from the Lord, but I give a judgment as one who by the Lord's mercy is trustworthy. . . . I think that. . . ." Here, too, Paul does not mean he is speaking merely from his own human understanding, but that he has no specific commandment from the lips of Jesus. Therefore, as *The Expositor's Greek New Testament* puts it, he is dealing here with "conditional advice" rather than a "peremptory rule."[6] In verse 40 he gives the qualification, "In my judgment . . . and I think that I too have the Spirit of God." Here again he is giving advice, not a command, hence the "judgment." As for thinking that he has the Spirit of God, to quote *Expositor's Greek New Testament* again, "It is the language of modesty, not of misgiving. The Apostle commends his advice in all these matters, conscious that it proceeds from the highest source and is not the outcome of mere human prudence or personal inclination."[7]

Thus, this passage as well as all of Paul's letters are the authoritative and binding Word of God.

## 1 Corinthians 7:3–5

In 1 Corinthians 7:3–5 Paul continues to point out that a husband and wife ought to have sexual relations with each other as their normal habit of life:

> The husband should fulfill his marital duty to his wife, and likewise the wife to her husband. The wife's body does not belong to her alone but also to her husband. In the same way, the husband's body does not belong to him alone but also to his wife. Do not deprive each other except by mutual consent and for a time, so that you may devote yourselves to prayer. Then come together again so that Satan will not tempt you because of your lack of self-control.

This is not an ascetic outlook, which views sexual relations even in marriage negatively, as if they are, at best, merely permissible or that sex is simply a necessary biological function for the purpose of procreation only. On the contrary, Paul insists that sex between husband and wife should be a matter of regular and normal enjoyment. Moreover, neither the one nor the other must claim the exclusive right to say yes or no in this matter; each must be subject to the other's desires as well.

## 1 Corinthians 7:8–9

Paul gives two options for the unmarried and widows in these verses: to remain unmarried or, if this is necessary to avoid sexual temptation, to marry. In what would the potential sexual temptation consist? The obvious implication is that it would be sexual relations outside of marriage, and these must include same-sex relations as well as fornication and adultery. It is difficult to believe that Paul would have considered a lesbian relationship an acceptable alternative for these women unless he had said so explicitly. Nor are we permitted to assume that the marriage he recommends could be a lesbian relationship without some hint of this possibility somewhere in the context.

### 1 Corinthians 7:10–16

First Corinthians 7:10–11 states that a husband and wife must not separate; but if they do, they should remain unmarried or else be reconciled to each other. This clearly excludes homosexual unions. In the contemporary scene, homosexual affairs are one of the causes of the break-up of marriages. Does Paul's failure to mention such unions specifically mean merely that homosexual unions are acceptable and subject to the same principle as normal marriages? Or does it imply that homosexual partners are free to do as they please in this matter of separation? Or must we conclude that Paul does not consider homosexual unions to be permissible?

Let us consider these three possibilities. First, Paul gives no hint elsewhere that he considers same-sex unions to be legitimate; so a specific mention of them would be required in order to include them here along with specifically mentioned heterosexual marriage. Second, he certainly could not feel that homosexual unions could be made and broken at the whim of one of the partners if this was not proper for husband-wife unions. Therefore, the only reasonable conclusion to be drawn from this passage of Scripture is that there is no place for homosexual unions in the Christian community.

The same argument applies to 1 Corinthians 7:12–16. Here Paul discusses the question of a Christian who is married to an unbeliever. Once again, nothing permits us to assume that Paul considers a same-sex union as legitimate for a Christian.

### 1 Corinthians 7:25–40

In these verses Paul discusses some problems of the married and the unmarried or widows. He goes into some detail in giving advice and expressing his concern. Once again we should remind ourselves that homosexuality was common in Corinth and in the Roman world in general. William Barclay, a well-known New Testament scholar, has noted that Greek society was thoroughly permeated with homosexuality. But even though it was nearly universal, "it was regarded as abnormal, and it was never legal."[8] Yet in the whole of 1 Corinthians 7 Paul gives no hint that the Corinthian Christians might engage in homosexual activity or homosexual unions as alternatives to, or in addition to, either marriage or celibacy. Verse 39 says that if a woman's husband dies, "she is free to marry anyone she wishes, but he must belong to the Lord." This permission does not include a possible lesbian relationship with another woman. Since Paul has nowhere given any indication that he considers a same-sex union to be permissible for Christians, no reasonable exegesis will permit the pronoun *anyone* here to include another woman.

## 1 Corinthians 11:11–12

Paul again emphasizes the exclusive man-woman relationship in 1 Corinthians 11:11–12: "In the Lord, however, woman is not independent of man, nor is man independent of woman. For as woman came from man, so also man is born of woman. But everything comes from God." It is wholly unwarranted to assume that Paul might well have added, "Although of course a woman may be joined to another woman and a man to another man in the Lord."

## Ephesians 5:22–33

In Ephesians 5:22–33 an exclusively husband-wife relationship is discussed. Paul points out that the wife should be subject to (this is not equivalent to being dominated by) her husband and points out much more extensively that the husband should love his wife with *agapē* love. He also adds the familiar reference from Genesis 2:24. If homosexual unions were proper, why did Paul not include such relationships in these exhortations?

We cannot assume that the principles Paul expresses in Ephesians 5:22–33 can tacitly be extrapolated to apply to homosexual unions. He nowhere gives any grounds for supposing that he includes homosexual unions in his thoughts on marriage relationships. In addition, the husband-wife roles and responsibilities as described here would not apply to a same-sex union; that would require a different orientation of roles.

### 1 Timothy 3:2, 12; 5:9

Paul states that an *episkopos* ("overseer") and a *diakonos* ("deacon") must be the "husband of one wife" (1 Tim. 3:2, 12 RSV; cf. Titus 1:6). While there are differences of interpretation of this phrase, it certainly prohibits sexual immorality. It means that a man must be true to his wife. The assumption is that he will usually be a married man, but there is no intention of disqualifying a bachelor, a widower, or a remarried widower, if their moral life is proper. There is no room for a homosexual option here. "Husband" and "wife" are specifically "man" (*anēr*) and "woman" (*gynē*)—designations that could hardly be extended to include a same-sex union. If Paul had wanted to allow for a homosexual relationship, he could have made a statement to that effect. The obvious conclusion is that these church officials were not permitted to engage in homosexual actions.

This argument is strengthened by a reference to 1 Timothy 5:9, which states that a widow, to be enrolled for aid from the church, must have been "the wife of one husband" (RSV), the converse of the preceding. Again, neither explicitly nor implicitly is there any basis for assuming that a lesbian partner would be considered an acceptable alternative to a husband. For both the men and the women included in these passages, moreover, the idea that homosexual activities were not mentioned merely because they were of no moral significance is simply inconceivable.

### Titus 2:4–5

In Titus 2:4–5 the older women of the church are instructed to teach the younger women to love their husbands (*philandrous einai*) and to be subject to their own husbands (*idiois andrasin*). Is there any room for a same-sex relationship here for these young women, either among themselves or with the older women who are assigned to teach them? The emphasis in this passage is quite the opposite: the norm for a young woman is to marry (a man), to love her husband, to be subject to him in the scriptural sense, and not to have any sexual involvement with anyone else of either sex.

## 1 Peter 3:1, 5, 7

In the same way, Peter emphasizes that women should be subject to their husbands and that husbands should be considerate of their wives (1 Peter 3:1, 5, 7). No allowance is made here for any sexual arrangements other than between husband and wife, and the clear implication of the context is that no alternative forms of "marriage" are acceptable.

## Hebrews 13:4

This verse states, "Marriage should be honored by all, and the marriage bed kept pure, for God will judge the adulterer and all the sexually immoral." Under the inspiration of the Holy Spirit, the author commends marriage and puts his approval on sexual relations in the bond of marriage. And he condemns heterosexual immorality. Does his silence concerning homosexual relations imply ignorance of such things, unconcern about them, or their tacit inclusion under "marriage"? He could not have been ignorant of something so common in the Greco-Roman world. He could hardly have remained silent because of unconcern; in such a case he would certainly have had to state that homosexuality was of no moral significance. And we have no reason to assume that *gamos* ("marriage") could have been understood by his readers to include a same-sex union.

## Jude 7

In this verse Jude states that "Sodom and Gomorrah and the surrounding towns gave themselves up to sexual immorality and perversion. They serve as an example of those who suffer the punishment of eternal fire." What this perversion was is clear from the story of the angels' deliverance of Lot and his family from the city of Sodom, which, along with the other cities of the plain, was destroyed by fire from God. They were guilty of homosexuality.

If I have seemed to belabor these passages, it has been for good reason. Advocates of homosexuality attempt to present same-sex relations as a permissible life style for Christians. Therefore, I have attempted to examine virtually every New Testament passage that deals with marriage and to show (1) that no form of permissible sexual union other than that of husband and wife is ever presented; (2) that many or most of these passages present the husband-wife relationship in a manner that implies exclusiveness—that is, there is no alternate permissible form of sexual union; and (3) that if same-sex unions were considered permissible, they most certainly would have been mentioned favorably or permissibly in at least a few of the passages that deal with marriage.

The issue of homosexual "marriages" is mentioned by Stan Roberts, pastor of the homosexually oriented Metropolitan Community Church in San Jose, California. Roberts says that his church performs same-sex "weddings," which they call "Holy Unions."[9]

To use the term *holy* for a homosexual union in a Christian frame of reference borders on blasphemy. The Greek word *hagios* ("holy") signifies that a person or thing is dedicated to a god for service and has qualities that reflect the character of the god in question. Thus, a god of war and violence could appropriately have a blood-stained warrior as a holy man, and a temple prostitute could appropriately be holy to a god of immorality and uncleanness. The God of the New Testament, however, is a God of absolute perfection and moral purity. Therefore, what is holy to Him must, in some reasonable manner, reflect His purity and perfection: inanimate sacrifices must be clean and undamaged, animals must be without physical blemish, and persons must in some real degree reflect His moral character in their lives. A homosexual union, then, contradicts the very principle on which God built the world and created its creatures and humanity. Such a union might indeed be "holy" to Satan or to a god of some of the world's tribal religions, but it is an abomination, the very opposite of holy, to the God of the New Testament.

In these passages my emphasis concerning homosexuality has been with particular regard to same-sex unions with some degree of permanence—unions that might bear some faint resemblance to marriage. I trust that it has become clear that in the New Testament such unions are nowhere, either explicitly or implicitly, presented as acceptable or permissible. It surely follows, then, much more certainly, that homosexual relations on a casual or impermanent basis are illegitimate. Even heterosexual relations, which are divinely approved and proper between husband and wife in marriage, are strictly forbidden outside of marriage, either between unmarried persons, in which case it is called fornication (*porneia*) or where one or both participants are married, in which case it is called adultery (*moicheia*). Both of these types of extramarital sexual activity are clearly prohibited by the New Testament (Matt. 5:27–28; Luke 18:20; Rom. 2:22; 1 Cor. 6:18; Eph. 5:3 et al.) Much more, then, would homosexual acts, which are not even permissible in a permanent relationship, be forbidden in a casual or promiscuous relationship.

### GREEK WORDS FOR HOMOSEXUALITY

Having examined the New Testament references to marriage and man-woman relationships to determine their implications for homosexual behavior, let us examine the terms by which the New Testament writers refer to homosexuality.

### Arsenokoitēs

The principal lexical item concerning same-sex activities is *arsenokoitēs* (in older Greek, *arrenokoitēs*). This word is found in the Sibylline Oracles and Diogenes Laertius, which means it is as old as the New Testament. It therefore reflects no credit on the objective scholarship of a clergyman such as John Boswell, who has stated that the word *homosexual* was not coined until the 1880s and that "ancient people did not distinguish between" homosexual and heterosexual persons. "Sexuality was sexuality," he declares.[10]

As to precisely when the English word *homosexual* originated, Boswell may be correct. But the ancient Greeks and Romans did not speak English! To take a supposed late date for this particular English word and conclude that the idea of homosexuality was unknown or undistinguished from heterosexual behavior in earlier times is something less than serious scholarship. Indeed, if this word was not used earlier in English, it was not due to a lack of discrimination but rather because homosexual behavior was considered so much more abhorrent than heterosexual immorality that writers hesitated to give it a specific name.

Even the King James Version of the Bible contradicts Boswell's claim. It translates the specific word for male homosexuality, *arsenokoitēs*, as "abusers of themselves with mankind" in 1 Corinthians 6:9 and as "them that defile themselves with mankind" in 1 Timothy 1:10. These phrases may seem obscure to our minds; but the very use of the euphemism rather than the explicit term—such as adultery, fornication, whoremonger, and harlot—in reference to heterosexual sins shows that the translators knew perfectly well what the term meant and that they considered it more degraded than adultery.

Matthew Poole published his *Annotations on the Holy Bible* in 1685. In regard to Romans 1:26 he says, "If they . . . that commit fornication dishonour their own bodies, then much more do they that practice the unnatural uncleanness hereafter mentioned." He goes on to refer to the homosexual acts mentioned here as "a filthy practice not to be named," although he did not hesitate to name fornication. On 1 Corinthians 6:9 he refers to the word for male homosexuality as describing "the sin of Sodom, a sin not to be named among Christians or men." Concerning the words *fornicators* (which here may mean immoral persons generally) and *male homosexuals*, he says, "[These] two terms express violations of the seventh commandment, whether by fornication, adultery, incest, sodomy, or any beastly lusts."[11] Does this sound as if Poole could not distinguish between heterosexual and homosexual sin?

John Albert Bengel's commentary, *Gnomon of the New Testament*, was first published in Latin in 1742 and was translated into English about 1857. In the discussion of the homosexual degradation described in Romans 1:26–27, Bengel uses no more specific words than "burned with an abominable fire . . . viz., of lust" and "that which is unseemly, against which the conformation of the body and its members [recoils]." In 1 Corinthians 6:9 he refers to homosexual behavior vaguely as "scandalous crimes," and in 1 Timothy 1:10 he passes over this same word.[12] S. T. Bloomfield, in his commentary of 1839, likewise avoids frank terms. Referring in Romans 1:26–27, he writes about "the dreadful corruption of morals in the ancient world." He also avoids a direct reference to "homosexuals" in 1 Corinthians 6:9 and 1 Timothy 1:10.[13]

Does this avoidance of explicit terms mean that these seventeenth-to-nineteenth-century authors did not know what homosexuality was or that they made no distinction between homosexual and heterosexual acts, as Dr. Boswell implies? On the contrary, these same writers have no hesitancy to use the words *fornication* and *adultery* and to point out the difference between these two terms where they find it appropriate. Their lack of frankness with reference to homosexual acts is due to the fact that they regarded these acts as so much more abominable and shameful than even adultery and fornication that they were reluctant to name them.

There remains, however, a gap of a good many centuries between the New Testament itself and the authors we have quoted. The comments on this subject by the ancient church fathers are discussed in the following chapter; but it may be well here to show that homosexuality was known and abhorred between the first and the seventeenth centuries as well as since then.

Thomas Aquinas lived from 1224 to 1274. In his *Summa Theologica* he refers to the "unnatural vice," including under this heading "autoeroticism" (which he calls "effeminacy"), "bestiality," and "sodomy" (under the latter he includes both male and female homosexuality). He further comments, "In every genus, worst of all is the corruption of the principle on which the rest depend. . . . Therefore, since by the unnatural vices man transgresses that which has been determined by nature with regard to the use of venereal [sexual] actions, it follows that in this matter this sin is gravest of all. After it comes incest." Further on, he says that in these homosexual acts, which are "sins contrary to nature, whereby the very order of nature is violated, an injury is done to God, the Author of nature."[14]

We may even bridge the period between Aquinas and the New Testament; for in the same discussion on homosexual sins, Aquinas continues by referring to Augustine (A.D. 354–430), stating, "Hence Augustine says (*Confessions* iii. 8): 'Those foul offenses that are against nature should be everywhere and at all times detested and punished, such as were those of the people of Sodom.'"[15]

This does not indicate that people in the fourth, fifth, thirteenth, seventeenth, eighteenth, and nineteenth centuries "did not distinguish between" heterosexual and homosexual actions and sins. Does it not rather reveal that certain apologists for homosexual license are shutting their eyes to disagreeable data?

To return to the Greek word under discussion, what is the meaning of *arsenokoitēs*? Liddell and Scott, in the unabridged edition of their standard Greek-English Lexicon (1843), declined to translate this word into English, giving only the Latin translation, *cinaedus*. The abridged edition (1871) of this lexicon, however, compromises Victorian standards sufficiently to render it as "one guilty of unnatural offenses," without further specifying the offenses. This manner of dealing with the word underlines the point made in the preceding paragraphs concerning the reluctance of earlier writers to name homosexuality specifically. Thayer's Greek-English Lexicon (1885) renders this word as "one who lies with a male as with a female, a sodomite." The more recent edition of Bauer, Arndt, and Gingrich's lexicon (1957) translates it as "a male homosexual, pederast, sodomite," citing this meaning in the ancient *Anthologia Palatina* and the *Catalogus Codicum Astrologorum Graecorum* and citing the related verb from the *Sibylline Oracles*.

There is no room for doubt concerning the meaning of *arsenokoitēs*. It is derived from *arsēn* (in older Greek, *arrēn*) ("a male") and *koitē* ("a bed"). With the suffix *-tēs* indicating the agent of an action, the etymology of the word is "a male-bed-person." The word *arsēn* puts emphasis on the aspect of gender or sex, in distinction both from *anēr* ("man" as distinct from woman) and *anthrōpos* ("man" or person generically). The second part of this word, *koitē,* is the ordinary word for "bed" (as in Luke 11:7, "my children are with me in bed"). From this primary sense the meaning is extended to the marriage bed (as in Hebrews 13:4, "the marriage bed kept pure"). The idiom *to have a bed* means to become pregnant, as in Romans 9:10; and the plural (beds) has the meaning of sexual excesses in Romans 13:13.

It is clear, then, that an *arsenokoitēs* in the New Testament is a man who goes to bed with a male for sexual purposes. This has been its accepted meaning ever since the time of ancient Greek literature. Even though only the one person, the male, is mentioned in this word, it has always been understood to mean male-with-male; it has never had the implication of a male going to bed with a female. To state, therefore, as does Boswell, that Paul's condemnations of homosexuality in the English New Testament are "blatant mistranslations," and "I doubt that

101

Paul had any concept of homosexuality as a separate category
of human beings," causes one to wonder at the obvious gaps in
Boswell's information.[16] The fact is that an ancient Greek, or a
modern scholar of ancient Greek, even if he were reading the
New Testament for the first time and had no previous knowledge of the New Testament or of Christian moral standards,
would have not the slightest difficulty in understanding the
meaning of this and the other terms we are discussing.

### Malakos

A second word that is relevant to our discussion is *malakos*.
The basic meaning of this word is "soft"; it is used in Matthew
11:8 and Luke 7:25 in a neutral sense of "soft clothing, such as
fastidious people wear" (Bauer, Arndt, and Gringrich, *Greek–
English Lexicon of the New Testament*). The same lexicon gives
*malakos* the further meaning of "soft, effeminate, especially
of catamites," the term *catamite* being defined as "men and
boys who allow themselves to be misused sexually," and citing instances of this meaning of the word from the Hibeh
Papyri of the late B.C. and early A.D. period, and from the
writings of Dionysius of Halicarnassus, Dio Chrysostom,
Vettius Valens, and Diogenes Laertius, of the first three Christian centuries.

*Malakos* in this moral sense is found in 1 Corinthians 6,
along with other words denoting sexual immorality: "Do you
not know that the wicked will not inherit the kingdom of God?
Do not be deceived: Neither the sexually immoral [*pornoi*] nor
idolaters nor adulterers [*moichoi*] nor male prostitutes
[*malakoi*] nor homosexual offenders [*arsenokoitai*] nor thieves
nor the greedy . . . will inherit the kingdom of God. And that is
what some of you were. But you were washed, you were
sanctified, you were justified in the name of the Lord Jesus
Christ and by the Spirit of our God" (vv. 9–11).

This Scripture could hardly have stated more clearly that
the Christians who had been guilty of homosexual behavior—as well as those who had been guilty of heterosexual sins,

stealing, drunkenness, and other sins—had been delivered by repentance and faith in Jesus Christ. The apostle says the believers were "washed . . . sanctified . . . justified." They no longer engaged in these sins; Paul says "you were," not "you are."

Dick Devor suggests that the apostle's condemnation of homosexuals in 1 Corinthians 6 and Romans 1 is also a condemnation of heterosexual persons since all men are under bondage to sin.[17] Of course all men are by nature under bondage to sin until they have been liberated by Christ, but that is not the point Paul is making in these passages. Instead, Paul is referring to certain specific acts that are sins and he is stating that persons who practice these sins cannot inherit the kingdom of God. His list of sins includes heterosexual acts outside of marriage and homosexual acts in general without restriction or qualification.

Paul sometimes condemns heterosexual sin, as he does in 1 Corinthians 6. However, in 1 Corinthians 6 and Romans 1 he does not say that people of whatever sexual orientation and conduct are sinners, implying that their sin was in some other area of life than their sexual activity. Yet this is what Devor is clearly maintaining. Rather, Paul is making it clear that sexual relations other than those between husband and wife are sinful and that people who engage in such activities are condemned by those specific acts.

Devor is clearly on the wrong track when he says, "The implication is that if Paul includes homosexuals, he includes heterosexuals. His point is that no one can claim righteousness by Law."[18] Paul does indeed clearly teach that no one can claim righteousness by law, but this is not his argument in 1 Corinthians 6:9–11. As for Devor's point that "if Paul includes homosexuals, he includes heterosexuals," this is absolutely contrary to what Paul is teaching here. It does no credit to Devor's understanding of the plain sense of the Greek text of the New Testament to make the application that he makes of this passage. The text clearly means that homosexual acts are per se sinful but that heterosexual acts are not sinful per se except outside of the marriage bond.

Nor can we avoid the weight of Paul's condemnation of homosexual acts by dragging out the red herring that it is possible to sin against one's own spouse through misuse of sex within the marriage bond. Some husbands and wives doubtless do sin against each other and against God by the misuse of sexual relations with each other. Such sins are worthy of condemnation. However, just as the fact that some persons have been harmed by misuse of water is no argument in favor of the use of alcohol, so instances of misuse of heterosexual relations do not alleviate the sinfulness of homosexual acts.

Neither an ancient Greek nor a modern scholar of the Greek language would have the slightest difficulty in understanding Paul's clear and obvious meaning in Romans 1:24–31 when he states, "Therefore God gave them over in the sinful desires of their hearts to sexual impurity [*akatharsia*] for the degrading of their bodies with one another. . . . Because of this, God gave them over to shameful lusts. Even [ both of the following things occurred (Gk. *te*)] their women [*thēleiai*] exchanged natural [*physikēn*] relations for unnatural ones. In the same way the men [*arsenes*] also abandoned natural relations with women and were inflamed with lust [*orexis*] for one another. Men committed indecent acts with other men, and received in themselves the due penalty for their perversion." Then, following a further list of sins of various types, he summarizes the degradation of these sinners by saying, "Although they know God's righteous decree [*dikaiōma*] that those who do such things deserve death, they not only continue to do these very things but also approve of those who practice them" (v. 32). How much more plainly could the Bible have declared that these men and women became involved in homosexual desires and behavior, and that such things, as well as other sins that are mentioned, are willful violations of the known will of God and are deserving of the punishment of death!

It is the sheerest trifling to attempt to circumvent the clear sense of this passage by appealing to the fact that Romans 1:27 refers to the males "leaving" the natural use of the female, as the King James Version puts it, and turning to homosexual actions—as if this Scripture condemns only the man who turns to homosexuality subsequent to heterosexual activity. (And where will one hear a condemnation of even this type of homosexuality by those who suggest such an interpretation?) In the present passage, "leaving" obviously refers to rejecting what is normal, whether the normal was first experienced or not. The same is true in regard to the reference in verse 26 that the females "exhanged" the natural use of their bodies for that which is contrary to nature, not necessarily meaning that what was normal had been experienced and then rejected in every instance.

*Arsenokoitēs* appears once more in the New Testament—in 1 Timothy 1:10: "We also know that law is made not for good men but for lawbreakers and rebels, the ungodly and sinful, the unholy and irreligious; for those who kill their fathers or mothers, for murderers, for adulterers [*pornoi*] and perverts [*arsenokoitai*], for slave traders and liars and perjurers—and for whatever else is contrary to the sound doctrine" (vv.9-10). To pretend that one of the actions involved in this dreary list, "perverts" (that is, homosexuals), is not totally and always wrong and sinful and that it may indeed be perfectly acceptable behavior for a Christian is simply to call clean what the New Testament calls unclean.

## Akatharsia

The word *akatharsia* ("uncleanness") itself, which is found in Romans 1:24, deserves attention, since in this verse it clearly refers to sexual immorality. This word and the related adjective *akathartos* ("unclean") may refer to physical, ceremonial, spiritual, or moral uncleanness. In Matthew 23:27 it is used, although figuratively, of the contents of graves, which produce ceremonial uncleanness for a Jew who touches them. In Romans 6:19 and 1 Thessalonians 2:3 it may have an ethical or spiritual significance. In the remaining six New Testament occurrences, it clearly refers to sexual immorality: 2 Corinthians 12:21, "impurity, sexual sin and debauchery"; Galatians 5:19, "sexual immorality, impurity and debauchery"; Ephesians 4:19, "sensuality . . . impurity"; Ephesians 5:3, "sexual immorality, or . . . any kind of impurity"; Colossians 3:5, "sexual immorality, impurity, lust, evil desires"; and 1 Thessalonians 4:7, at the end of a passage concerning sexual ethics, "For God did not call us to be impure, but to live a holy life."

In summary, the words and passages we have been studying self-evidently classify all homosexual behavior as immoral, as well as all heterosexual relations outside of marriage. Only the incredible denials of these clear implications by defenders of homosexual life styles keep this discussion from being a repetitious belaboring of the obvious.

In the larger scope of this discussion, it has become clear that the New Testament (1) supports and advocates marriage between a man and a woman and regards sexual relations between husband and wife as right and proper both for procreation and for the expression of love and unity in marriage; (2) condemns as sinful and abhorrent these same sexual relations between a man and a woman under any circumstances except within marriage and does so without exception; and (3) condemns as sinful any kind of homosexual relations, either male or female, under any circumstances, whether casual or permanent, and does so without exception.

### HOMOSEXUALITY AND PERSONAL RESPONSIBILITY

It should be carefully noted that to say that the New Testament condemns homosexual actions is not to say that it explicitly condemns homosexuality as a personal tendency. When we use the terms *homosexual* and *homosexuality* in a context of condemnation, it should be understood that we are referring to homosexual behavior and not to homosexual tendencies. It is not within the province of this chapter to deal with the origin of homosexual tendencies. However, it would certainly be inconsistent with the righteous character of the God who is revealed to us in the New Testament to condemn what is simply the natural behavior of a person as God has created him. Both the New Testament's presentation of an exclusively male-female concept of sexuality and its categorical condemnation of homosexual behavior every time such behavior is mentioned clearly imply that homosexuality is not, like heterosexuality, a gift of God.

Let us suppose, for argument's sake, that it can be shown that some persons have a "natural" tendency toward homosexuality. Even this would not prove that homosexuality is created by God and is therefore a life style that is acceptable to Him. Consider the universal tendency toward sin in general, from which no person is free in his natural condition. Shall we pronounce this condition God-given and declare that a life of sinning is therefore a divinely approved way of life for the Christian, since he was born with this tendency? Following such a pattern, should we not help the alcoholic secure enough alcohol to satisfy his "natural" desire? Should we not help the kleptomaniac satisfy his proclivity to stealing, and the psychotic killer his compulsion to kill?

The fact is, of course, that we should not be surprised if the condition in which we are born differs from the condition in which man was created by God. Genesis 2–3 describe a well-known incident in the Garden of Eden that distorted God's image, not only in our first parents but in all their descendants as well. From that moment until the present, it has been more "natural" for human beings to sin than to live in holiness. But this neither excuses nor legitimizes even one person's yielding to this sinful nature and continuing in a life of sin.

As a part of the resultant depravity in the human heart and mind—a depravity that infected every area of life—the sexual aspect was distorted. This beautiful gift of God for husband and wife became twisted to include Satan's parodies of sex—fornication, adultery, homosexuality, bestiality, and other aberrations.

Nevertheless, whatever the origin of homosexual tendencies, the New Testament condemns homosexual actions. This condemnation, of course, extends to the desire to commit the act (as distinct from mere temptation), just as the desire to commit adultery is condemned as the equivalent of the adulterous act. This means that a person with homosexual tendencies is expected to resist the temptation to homosexual activity by the help of the Holy Spirit, just as an unmarried person is expected to resist the temptation to commit fornication and as a married person is expected to resist the temptation to commit adultery.

If a person fails to resist the temptation that comes to him and commits sin—be it homosexual, heterosexual, or any other type of sin—God's grace offers him the opportunity to repent and be forgiven. First John 2:1-2 assures us, "If anybody does sin, we have one who speaks to the Father in our defense—Jesus Christ, the Righteous One. He is the atoning sacrifice for our sins."

To expect a person, with divine help, to resist homosexual tendencies is not the harsh and unequal treatment it is claimed to be by some defenders of homosexuality. Heterosexually oriented persons are likewise commanded by the New Testament to refrain from sexual actions, both in thought and deed, except within the marriage bond. All of us know perfectly well that many persons, both men and women, including some who make no claim to be Christians, go through life without sexual experience and that many married persons who are separated from their spouses for periods of time can and do keep themselves free from sexual involvement during those times. Yet how many of these people have not been subjected to sexual temptation, and even sexual opportunity, at some time? If there is victory over heterosexual temptations, especially with the divine resources available to the Christian, then victory is surely possible over tendencies to homosexual sins as well. This is the promise of 1 Corinthians 10:13, "No temptation has seized you except what is common to man. And God is faithful;

he will not let you be tempted beyond what you can bear. But when you are tempted, he will also provide a way out so that you can stand up under it."

This struggle with homosexual tendencies, from a Christian viewpoint, is well presented in a book entitled *The Returns of Love*. It is a collection of letters written anonymously by a Christian young man who has homosexual tendencies. With divine help, he resists these tendencies and seeks to bring himself to a normal heterosexual life. At one point this young man writes that a homosexual cannot plead before God, "I couldn't help it," because "somewhere along the line his passive submission to sin must have been a matter of active choice, and for that action he is held responsible."[19]

## GOD CREATED TWO SEXES

Perhaps the charge that sex acts other than heterosexual are parodies of sex warrants some further explanation. It was not accidental that Jesus specified that the Creator made them "male and female" (Matt. 19:4) and not "man and woman." He was, of course, quoting the Old Testament, and the argument can be extended to the Old Testament passage as well. But Jesus could have paraphrased or softened the Old Testament statement had He so desired. "Male and female" here (*arsēn* and *thēlys*) deliberately focus on the two distinct sexes. The implication is that the two sexes are intended to complement each other. If this Scripture passage does not specifically rule out sexual relationships other than male-female, it at least clearly implies that God's intention for sex from the beginning of the human race was male-female and nothing else.

The joining of a husband and wife, the male with the female, Jesus declares, produces a unity in which the male and the female are no longer two but one flesh. Each of the two was, in a sense, a half. The explicit phrase *male and female* suggests that these two halves are not identical halves but complementary halves. Genesis 2:18 does not say that God decided to create an identical twin for Adam but a "helper suitable for him," a complementary person. The union is thus not made like the two halves of a circle but is perhaps better understood by the analogy of a pair of shoes. To attempt to make a union of two females or two males is not to make a united whole but rather a repetition of identical halves. The result compares to a "pair" of two left-foot shoes, or a person with a right hand on each arm.

Someone may argue that in Galatians 3:28 Paul supports the idea of the obliteration of sex distinctions for Christians. This is hardly correct. Paul is simply arguing that persons are equal in Christ's sight and in His sacrifice and that no one is preferred above nor debased below another—neither Jew nor Greek, slave nor free, male nor female. The distinct classes and identities obviously remain, but they are not to be made the basis of privilege or lack of privilege in Christ. The Greek text, rather literally translated, reads, "There is [emphatically] not Jew nor Greek, there is [emphatically] not slave nor free, there is [emphatically] not male and female; for you are all one person in Christ Jesus."

### The "Right" to Sexual Fulfillment

The pressure for the satisfaction of the sexual appetite without regard to marriage comes, in large measure, from the sexual stimulation to which many people permit themselves to be subjected. There are also the stimuli that are thrust on them unwittingly—in print, in the theater, on television, by others' immodest dress, and in other ways. The stimulation naturally leads to a desire for satisfaction, just as the aroma of a broiling steak stimulates the desire for food in a person who has not eaten for several hours.

The New Testament speaks to this point as well. Warning us against permitting ourselves to be sexually stimulated to a point where sexual desire is aroused, Jesus states that not only is the act of adultery sinful, but "anyone who looks at a woman lustfully has already committed adultery with her in his heart" (Matt. 5:28).

If we accept the unbiblical premise that every person is entitled to sexual activity, then it may appear to follow reasonably that if a person's inclinations are homosexual, he has the right to homosexual activity. What this line of argument fails to admit, however, is the clear implication that if the desire and the inclination legitimize the expression, then not only homosexual behavior is legitimate but also fornication, adultery, and bestiality. None of these may logically be excluded on the grounds given. This type of argument may make good humanism, with man the measure of all things. But it is a far cry from the biblical standard of holiness and purity, which reflects God's holiness in every aspect of life based on the admonition, "Be holy because I, the Lord your God, am holy" (Lev. 19:2).

One of our problems is that this assumption is commonly presented as valid. Professing Christians let it be forced into their minds until they begin to feel that chastity is a losing battle and biblical standards are too idealistic to be maintained or are even irrelevant.

The liberationists' declaration, however, is the big lie. The Bible insists on a standard of sexual morality that can be maintained. Countless multitudes have maintained it through the ages and still do, including people of diverse cultures and many who have never heard of the Bible's teachings.

### CAN'T I DO AS I PLEASE WITH MY BODY?

Does not a person have the right to do as he wishes with his own body? The biblical reply is no. The non-Christian reply might seem to be yes, but even the non-Christian can really go no further than a qualified "Yes, but. . . ."

To illustrate this principle, suppose a man buys a new Cadillac and pays the full price in cash. He drives his luxury car home and finds the owner's manual in the glove compartment. He begins to read the instructions, and the more he reads, the more indignant he becomes. Finally, he takes to his typewriter and drafts a letter to General Motors:

Dear Sirs:

I have just purchased one of your expensive Cadillacs, paying cash at the time of purchase. Upon reaching home, I find in the car an owner's manual in which you tell me what to do and not do with my car.

Let me make one thing clear. You have no further claim on this car. It is completely mine. I refuse to permit you or anyone else to dictate to me how I should take care of my own property. I am returning your owner's manual to you to give to someone who is stupid enough to believe that you can still control your product after you have sold it.

This man then proceeds to do as he pleases with his new car. He decides that water is perfectly good for the crankcase instead of motor oil. He drives his car through his farmland, hitting boulders and running through ditches. He refuses to check the air pressure in the tires.

General Motors has no legal right or power to interfere with this mistreatment of a fine car. The owner handles his car as he chooses. However, he cannot avoid the consequences of his choice, which is the ruin of his automobile.

Similarly, a person can do as he pleases with his body; God has given him that privilege. However, the person must also accept the consequences of his choice. The consequences are a part of the cause-and-effect relationships of the universe, as is implied in passages such as Romans 1:27.

The Christian's position is, *I do not have the unrestricted right to do as I please with my body.* This response is based on the biblical principle of stewardship, as in 1 Corinthians 6:19-20: "Do you not know that your body is a temple of the Holy Spirit, who is in you, whom you have received from God? You are not your own; you were bought at a price. Therefore honor God with your body."

Indeed, the Christian point of view is that God has a double claim on the person and his body. God has not only the claim by redemption but also, from the beginning, the claim of creation. It is God who "from one man . . . made every nation of men" (Acts 17:26) and "from whom his whole family in heaven and on earth derives its name" (Eph. 3:14). The biblical viewpoint is, therefore, that God has a right to expect us to care for our bodies in accordance with His instructions because we belong to Him. In addition, however, we ought to obey His instructions about the care of our mind and body because He created us and best knows how we should live.

In short, we ought to live according to certain principles because these principles correspond to the nature of the real world and because they represent the Creator's will for us. These principles are given to us in the Bible, and they are both correct and a moral obligation to us.

Even the non-Christian, if he believes in God as Creator, should logically assume that if God has given guidelines for life, everyone would be wise to follow those guidelines. The person who rejects the idea of God has no sure guidelines for his life and may therefore grasp at all sorts of substitutes for the "owner's manual." If, however, it is true that God is the Creator, then God's guidelines are valid and His warnings are based on fact, whether the person accepts them or not.

Accepting God's laws as both correct and morally binding, the Christian will believe that there are some things he has no right to do with his body, and that there are things two persons have no right to do together even if they are mutually willing. This principle should not be regarded as an anomaly; it is recognized in other areas of life that there are two levels of ownership. For example, under our laws a person can be charged with the crime of arson if he burns down his own house, even if it is fully paid for and he has no insurance benefits to claim. A farmer on the northern Minnesota border has no legal right to secede from the United States and give his farm to Canada. Even more personally, our government tells us that, under penalty of the law, we may not take certain substances into our body and calls it a crime for one to take his own life.

In a similar and profound way, God has a claim on us and our bodies—a claim we cannot ultimately avoid. His laws, moreover, are not the mere whims of an arbitrary dictator; they are the principles on which the universe was created and on which it operates. When a person says with the psalmist, "To do your will, O my God, is my desire," he is living in accordance with the nature of things and in obedience to a God of absolute love and perfect holiness who could never want anything less than the best for His children.

# 3

# The Church Fathers and Homosexuality

The author is a doctoral student at the Catholic University of Louvain in Louvain, Belgium, and is specializing in oriental patristics. He is a graduate of Seattle Pacific College, where he received his B.A. degree, and Asbury Theological Seminary, where he received his M.Div. and Th.M. degrees. Mr. Bundy is the author of Keswick: A Bibliographic Introduction to the Higher Life Movements and has contributed articles to various theological periodicals. He is a member of the following professional associations: Society of Biblical Literature, American Academy of Religion, North American Patristic Society, and Wesleyan Theological Society.

## By David D. Bundy

# Homosexuality

in the Old Testament
in the New Testament
**in church history**
in the physical and emotional
in the courtroom
in the church

**3** How should the church respond to homosexuality? This is perhaps the most difficult question facing the church in our day. It is an issue that, to be answered responsibly, requires us to reexamine our ideas about sin, mankind, and the Bible. In such a quest, every resource available to inform our decisions needs to be utilized. One resource that has been little used is that of the collective wisdom of our predecessors in the faith, that is, the fathers, or great teachers, of the church. This is the case primarily because the volumes written by those who wish to remove all theological and ecclesiastical stigma from homosexuality and homosexual relationships have found the material incompatible with their position. Their judgment is that the early Christian writers were uninformed men who were overly influenced by their culture and misunderstood the intent of the apostle Paul. This opinion has been uncritically accepted by many other writers, but it simply is not true. The church fathers were often recognized as among the best minds of their eras. Their world was different from ours, but their articulation of their views did not lack in sophistication. They were earnest Christians who took seriously their responsibility to mediate the faith of the apostles to their age.

Who were these church fathers? Clement of Alexandria stated in the second century, "We call 'Fathers' those who have instructed us in the Faith."[1] They are not merely the subjects of innumerable tales recorded in oversized books with dusty-leather or dull-cloth covers. They were ordinary and extraordinary people who experienced an awakening of faith and sought by the power of the Spirit of God working through them to mediate that faith by making the message of Christian hope and love real to their world. They were real persons who struggled with pressing problems of life and faith and death. They never claimed infallibility for their solutions to given dilemmas, yet their fearlessness and honesty demands we hear them. They did not always agree with one another. Yet, their goals were the same. They sought to communicate faith in Christ. The story of the dreams and defeats, idealism and cynicism, fidelity and

117

infidelity, and consistency and inconsistency of our forerunners in the faith is what the study of the Fathers is all about.

Not only does the Christian have a genetic and social heritage passed down from generations past, but he also has "roots" in twenty centuries of Christian faith. From the beginning, the apostles told their story and some of their hearers believed. These in turn told others. Finally someone told the story of Christ to you and me with its attendant implications for our lives. These are our spiritual roots. These are our fathers in the faith. In this study we specifically refer to the early church fathers and their writings.

We will consult the Fathers at only one point: to discover what they had to say about homosexuality and homosexual relationships. To achieve an understanding of their perspective, it is necessary to ask, What did they say? But it is imperative that we go beyond this level of interrogation to inquire on what basis of authority they argued and why they spoke as they did.

We shall limit our inquiry to the most important writers of the first five centuries of the Christian era. This period is particularly significant for our investigation since the mother tongue of most of these authors was Greek. Thus, although language changes, they read the Scriptures from a linguistic background and world view far more similar to those of the first Christian century than are ours today. Also, during the first three centuries, the Christian writers were trying to establish what it meant to be a disciple of Christ in an era generally inhospitable to the Christian faith. During the next two centuries, they were forced to deal with imperial politics, which were summarily injected into the church.

Let us examine the writings of each of these periods in turn. The names of the authors may seem strange (if you pronounce them as they appear, you will be relatively accurate). But don't allow the unfamiliarity of the name to rob you of what that person may be able to contribute to your understanding of your Christian heritage.

## ESTABLISHING A CHRISTIAN IDENTITY

During the first three centuries of the Christian era, the teachers of the church were concerned with articulating what it means to be a Christian. What do Christians believe? How do those who have accepted that faith act? This quest was necessitated by forces both within and outside of the community of faith. Governmental authorities continually received accusations about the behavior of Christians. The success of a tract endeavoring to exonerate them could mean the difference between toleration and persecution. Also, those who had experienced the reality of the risen Christ in their own lives needed guidance to withstand the temptations to accept patterns of behavior incongruous with the New Testament faith. The early writers sought to meet this need with letters, theological essays, and apologies (defenses) of Christianity.

The Christians of this period lived in two worlds. The one was pagan. The materialism and idolatry of that world was incompatible with the world they had discovered in Jesus Christ. This was emphatically true of the sexual ethics of the Roman world. Though the church fathers often disagreed about other issues, they generally present a united voice concerning sex and social ethics, of which homosexuality was but one facet. They often quoted Romans 1:26–27; 1 Corinthians 6:9–11; and 1 Timothy 1:9–11 as summaries of sinful activities. There is no doubt that they understood these lists to include homosexuality. The unanimity at this point among the earliest Christian literary sources available strongly suggests that there is no justification for recent claims that Paul could not have proscribed homosexual activity.

### In the Second Century

The first extant appropriations of the Pauline sin lists are from the first half of the second century. Polycarp (c. 70–c. 155) was a prominent Christian leader in Asia Minor. Threatened with death, he refused to renounce Christ and so suffered mar-

tyrdom. Polycarp's letter to the church at Philippi is an important witness to the concerns of the second-generation
Christians. In this letter he quoted 1 Corinthians 6:9–10 in the
midst of an injunction to young Christian men to live a virtuous
life. He concluded, "Let the younger men be blameless in all
things." Because those who commit iniquity will not inherit
the kingdom of God, "it is necessary to refrain from all these
things and to be subject to the presbyters and deacons as to God
and Christ."[2]

*The Teaching of the Twelve Apostles,* written between 100
and 150, is a manual for the instruction of Christians seeking to
live in a Christian way. The author, whose identity is not
known, says that life presents two alternatives: the way of life
and the way of death. The way of life has both positive and
negative aspects. The positive is formulated in terms of love for
God and neighbor. It was to be a second-mile Christianity. The
negative is a list of practices to be avoided: "You shall not
commit murder, you shall not commit adultery, you shall not
commit homosexual acts, you shall not steal."[3]

Another ancient document constitutes one of the most win-
some introductions to Christian faith and the church ever
written. *The Epistle to Diognetus* does not explicitly mention
homosexuality, but it does concur with the other early Christian writings with respect to sexual purity in general. The writer of this beautiful essay informs his readers that Christians
"marry as all men, they bear children but do not expose [with
the intent to kill] their offspring. They offer free hospitality, but
guard their purity."[4]

God has committed a great responsibility to Christians.
They are to be a new people. Therefore, it is not right for them
to depreciate their responsibility.

Bardesanes was a philosopher-theologian of early-second-
century Edessa on the eastern frontier of the Roman Empire.
Later generations would judge his theology as not sufficiently
orthodox, but in his time he was a persuasive defender of
Christianity.

His *Book of the Laws of the Countries* is a report of a dialogue between Bardesanes and one of his students. The student had argued that all was controlled by fate. He contended that man is not responsible for his behavior. Bardesanes, as a Christian, refused to accept this evaluation of human nature. It is true, he argued, that man is limited by his human nature. He is born, grows toward adulthood, engenders children, and dies. He cannot change these things, just as he cannot continue to live if he refuses all food and drink. However, God has granted mankind the freedom to make moral decisions. The commandments of God may be followed or ignored. Each person, irrespective of wealth, health, or personal characteristics, has that prerogative and responsibility.

As proof of this contention, Bardesanes chronicles the social norms of the different countries, discussing Britain, India, and nations in between. Each country has its particular laws and abuses. In each country the people submit to the laws and norms imposed upon them. How do the Christians, "that the Messiah has caused to arise in every place and in all climates," then live? He suggests that the Christians follow the law of the Messiah. In all lands they are known by one name. They are of different social classes but have a common ethic.

> On the first day of the week we gather together and on the appointed days we abstain from food. And our brothers who live in Gaul, [contrary to local custom] do not marry with men, and they who live in Parthia do not marry two women . . . they who live in Persia do not marry their daughters . . . those who live in Edessa do not kill their wives or sisters. . . . Local custom cannot force them to give up the law of their Messiah, nor does fate . . . force them to do things that are unclean for them.[5]

Bardesanes most certainly considered homosexuality and other sexual abuses to be non-Christian and pagan practices.

Aristides, a resident of the city of Athens, was described by one of his contemporaries as a "man of faith" devoted to Christianity. His arguments insisting on the integral relation of faith and actions have been preserved in *An Apology in Behalf of* the Christians. He argued that the fact that the Greeks and barbarians worshiped decadant deities led them to involvement in sinful activities. The Christians, however, worshiped the one true God. This fact manifested itself in the way the Christians lived. The Christians were a people who cared for each other's needs. They gave so that others might live. They did not exploit anyone. They did not become involved in idolatry, pagan legal proscriptions, homosexuality, or adultery. They seriously tried to avoid greed.

His description of Christian behavior is a tribute to the church of the second century:

> They have the commandments of the Lord Jesus Christ himself graven upon their hearts and these they observe, looking for the resurrection of the dead and for the life in the world to come. They do not commit adultery nor fornication, nor do they bear false witness. . . . They comfort those who do wrong to them and make friends of them. They are eager to do good to their enemies. They are meek and gentle. They refrain from all unlawful intercourse and from all impurity. They do not despise the widow and oppress not the orphan. He that has gives ungrudgingly to him that has not. . . . For they call themselves brethren not after the flesh but after the spirit.[6]

Tatian also wrote a book in defense of Christianity. In his *Discourse to the Greeks* he defines and argues for a Christian world view. He examines the nature of the universe, of demons, of contemporary Greek culture, and of the moral value of Christianity. Tatian says that we become like what we worship. Sin is due to abuse of our free will and reflects the nature of the divinity we in reality worship. Since the God of the Christians is who He is, "there ought to be one code of behavior for all."[7] Tatian observed that the Romans encouraged homosexual practices while others, notably certain of the "barbarians," rejected homosexuality but practiced other forms of sexual abuse. The Christians were different. They were to be indifferent to social class and social station. They were not to value persons on the basis of wealth. All that rested on human opinion was rejected. "Persons of every age are treated by us with respect. They do not do as the Romans who sexually abuse young boys. Every kind of licentiousness is kept at a distance."[8]

Athenagoras of Athens was a contemporary of Tatian. We know almost nothing of his personal life but are fortunate to have *The Supplication for the Christians*, which he wrote about 177 and addressed to some of the Roman emperors. Athenagoras wrote to set the record straight concerning three charges made against the Christians: (1) atheism, (2) cannibalism, and (3) sexual perversion. In discussing sexual morality, he contended that the pagans themselves were guilty even of homosexuality, which is to be viewed as a form of social exploitation. That is, "the stronger chase the weaker, and in fact this is to feed upon human flesh."[9] Homosexuality was, for him, a form of social cannibalism. Sexual abuse—adultery, homosexual behavior, and abortion—is seen as evidence of a lack of appreciation for human life and thus incompatible with the Christian world view. Sexual purity, said Athenagoras, is to be maintained within the Christian community even on the level of the individual's thought life.

Theophilus of Antioch was the sixth bishop of that city. He himself had received an excellent classical education. Not until he was an adult did he become confronted with and accept the claims of Christianity. *Ad Autolycum*, his only extant writing, is a three-volume defense of Christianity in light of the objections of his pagan friend Autolycus. As was common among the early defenders of Christianity, he concerned himself with the nature of God, man's relationship to divinity, and morality.

God is visible only to those who have had opened the "eyes of the soul" and who maintain this condition of purity. "Just as a man must keep a mirror polished, so must he keep his soul pure."[10] Those who would see God must, in the words of 2 Corinthians 7:1, cleanse themselves "from everything that contaminates." In the list presented by Theophilus, that includes both active and passive homosexual behavior.

The Pauline sin list is cited again by Theophilus in the

123

context of asserting that it is essential that Christian faith, guided by the prophetic writings, manifest itself in obedience to God. Certain sexual activities will lead to present condemnation as well as to future anguish:

> But to the unfaithful who disregard and disobey the truth but obey unrighteousness, when they are full of adultery, and fornications and homosexual acts and greed and lawless idolatry, there will be wrath, tribulation and anguish and finally eternal fire will overtake such men.[11]

Theophilus was also scandalized by the approval of homosexual acts by the Stoics and Epicurus and disapproved of other philosophers who condoned other forms of sexual promiscuity. He summarized the Christian perspective:

> Monogamy is preserved, purity is guarded; injustice is driven out, sin is uprooted, righteousness is practiced, law is the guiding principle, piety is performed, God is acknowledged; truth controls, grace preserves, peace protects; holy logos leads, Sophia teaches, life controls, God reigns.[12]

### In the Third Century

In the following century, the nature of Christian literature changed drastically. It became generally more sophisticated in argumentation, richer in literary style, and more cognizant of the multifaceted nature of the cultural matrix in which the writers lived. The first great writer of the third century was Clement of Alexandria (150?–215). Born, perhaps in Athens, to pagan parents, his lifelong search for truth led him eventually to Alexandria where he studied and where he succeeded his professor as director of the school for new Christians. He became an influential teacher, thinker, and scholar who sought to define a Christian approach to the problems of the world and to the issues confronting the Christian church.

At the end of a defense of the sanctity of Christian marriage, Clement in his work *Stromateis*[13] urged sexual purity against a rationalism characterized by its sexual licentiousness. He reminds his readers of the words of Titus 1:15: "To the pure, all things are pure, but to those who are corrupted and do not believe, nothing is pure. In fact, both their minds and consciences are corrupted." First Corinthians 6:9–11 is quoted as a list of illicit indulgences. These, Clement observed, become the focal point of a participant's life, with the result that he puts himself outside God's kingdom. Such people "deprive themselves of enrolment as disciples," and follow the road to outer darkness. He contrasted this with "whatever is true . . . whatever is pure," quoting Philippians 4:8.

Clement thus argued that purity of sexual behavior on the Pauline model is a prerequisite both for usefulness in the present kingdom and for involvement in the kingdom to come. Self-control and a set of priorities that lead to the peace of God are Christian obligations. The orientation of a Christian's free will is all-important in the reclamation and restoration of the image of God in persons. The physical processes of creation and procreation are not bad in themselves. They lead to outer darkness only when people pervert them.

Another of Clement's writings is *The Instructor*. This volume was a manual for Christians in which the author sought to delineate a Christian ethic in practical terms. It does not reflect a blind legalism. Each suggestion is developed on the basis of the biblical texts with documentation of the consequences of a life style that is contrary to the Christian ethic. Careful reasons are given for his contentions, which cover everything from personal care to social behavior. This is done in such graphic terms that the early translators were embarrassed! So much so, indeed, that entire chapters were translated into Latin to make them accessible to scholars only! Clement was no ivory-tower scholar!

As a part of his discussion of proper behavior for men, Clement laments homosexual acts. He gives three reasons. First, he feels sympathy for those who are seduced, abused, and misused. He especially objects to the apparently common practice of holding youth in slavery to satisfy the perverted pleasure of the rich. Second, the behavior pattern of homosexuality is considered contrary to nature. Finally, it is a symptom and logical, if undesirable, outgrowth of excessive desire for the luxurious and the sensuous, a result of social disorder and a contributory factor to further degeneration. Christian love is to avoid licentiousness and exploitation.

The Christian is to follow the evangelical precepts and strive toward a spiritual and moral perfection worthy of a participant in the kingdom of God. If that is not our goal, we need to heed the admonitions of God that have been given us in the previous judgments of history. Clement is perhaps the earliest Christian author to suggest that Sodom was a judgment and an instruction for those who follow. It is important to note that, contrary to recently published claims, Clement perceived homosexuality to have been but one facet of a more general sinful condition in Sodom. He observed that because of a preoccupation with luxury and licentious living, the Sodomites merited the punishment they received.

Clement's successor at Alexandria was his student Origen (c. 185–c. 254). This man was a fervent Christian. At eighteen years of age he became the director of the school for new Christians in Alexandria when Clement was forced into exile during a period of persecution. Origen developed into a brilliant scholar who was as concerned about consistent Christian life style as about the theoretical questions of theological study.

Origen alluded to homosexuality in the context of a discussion of temptation in his book *On Prayer*. He proposed that God does not give us over to temptation with the intent that we should succumb. God does not direct anyone to evil. "God orders every rational soul with a view to eternal life . . . it always maintains its free will and of its own direction either mounts ever higher and higher until it reaches a pinnacle of virtue, or on the contrary descends through carelessness to this or that excess of wickedness."[14] If persons persist in sinful activities, they become ensnared by their sin, "exchang[ing] the glory of the immortal God for images made to look like mortal man . . ." (Rom. 1:23).[15] And thus being of a "depraved mind," they turn to sexual and other social exploitation.

Another of Origen's writings, *The Dialogue With Heraclides,* is a record of a discussion at a church synod. The orthodoxy of a bishop was in question, and Origen was asked to explain the fine points of theology involved. In response to a question posed by one of the participants about the power of God in the beyond as well as in the present world, Origen claimed that although the details of divine personality and action were beyond his understanding, it is attested in Scripture that salvation is for the entire person—body, soul, and spirit. Then he said,

> We must realise that at the divine tribunal we are not judged for faith alone, as if our life were left unexamined, nor for our life alone, as if our faith were not subject to scrutiny. We are justified on the ground that both are correct. . . . If then we wish to be saved led us not be concerned about faith to the neglect of practical conduct of life.[16]

This concern includes both "sins of life or of thought" and those considered by some Christians to be less important. Here he cites 1 Corinthians 6:9–11 where the homosexual person is listed among those who will not inherit the kingdom of God.

## In the Fourth Century

Athanasius (296–373), a key person in Christian history, lived through the period of transition of Christianity from the faith of a persecuted group of believers to a legal, recognized religion. The works mentioned here were written, most probably, about 318. Labeled by one of his contemporaries as "the pillar of the church," Athanasius often stood alone as the champion of orthodoxy in the face of Arian political and ecclesiastical challenges. Not even five banishments from his church in Alexandria by imperial authorities could dampen his ardor or devotion to what he perceived to be the crucial elements of faith.

In the midst of his struggle, Athanasius found time to write several books and many tracts. One of his compositions is a volume in two parts known as *Against the Heathen* and *The Incarnation of the Word*. It is instructive that in each section the problems of homosexuality and other sexual abuses are discussed. In *Against the Heathen* he developed the thesis that Christianity is much more reasonable than paganism. He discussed at length the historical development of pagan theologies and analyzed the behavior attributed to those gods. He concluded that after mankind became controlled by unreasonable passions and pleasures, people were unable to perceive the possibility of any other life style. Therefore, they fashioned the divine in the image of their own wickedness and used this false image of God as a rationale for devoting themselves to their own desires. Those not satisfied with their physical and social roles used this theology as permission for their licentiousness, including homosexuality, which Athanasius described by quoting Romans 1:26–27.

*The Incarnation of the Word* provided quite a different context for a discussion of homosexuality. In this volume, Athanasius sought to explicate the purpose of the incarnation, death, and resurrection of Christ. "The Lord came among us" because of the fallen state of mankind. God had created man incorruptible and "willed that he should remain in incorruptibility."[17] He continued, "For God did not only create us from nothing, but he also granted us by the grace of the word to live a divine life." However, mankind, "by the counsel of the devil," corrupted that pristine purity. People turned against nature and indulged in sin, becoming "insatiable in sinning."[18] Homosexuality is listed as a sin by which men and women turned against nature and against the divine plan for their lives. For Athanasius, to be involved in homosexual behavior was to abrogate the purpose both of the creation and of Christ's advent into the world.

### EDUCATING A "CHRISTIAN" EMPIRE

The radically changed legal status of Christianity following the reforms of Emperor Constantine (312–337) presented the church fathers with new challenges. No longer were they strangers to the halls of imperial power. No longer were they leaders of a select community, most of whose members had chosen to align themselves with the church because of a faith encounter with the Christian claims. Suddenly Christianity had become a state religion. Not only did it become popular to join the church, it also became politically and socially prudent. It was impossible for the local teachers to instruct all new adherents in the faith and to integrate them into a community with a clearly defined ethos. Thus, the empire became more or less synonymous with the church. Pagan feasts, practices, and temples were "baptized" and the ethos of the empire became the popular ethos of the church.

The church fathers of the fourth and fifth centuries approached their monumental task with great dedication and enthusiasm. Preaching became increasingly important. It was the only way in which to address and instruct large groups. It is no accident that most of the great teachers of the following two centuries were also well known for their preaching abilities.

Nor was the responsibility of the Fathers any longer limited to the confines of the church. They had been given standing in the larger social matrix. Therefore they felt themselves responsible to influence society so that it might be more just and humane.

## Reforming the Laws

Roman society was based, to a large extent, on a respect for law, and therefore the Christian leaders actively sought to change and reform those laws. The Roman emperors had long frowned on homosexuality. From early times there had been laws on the books, albeit apparently rarely enforced, prohibiting homosexual acts. However, under the aegis of the "Christian" emperors, the laws were made more explicit and often provided with a rationale based on Christian teachings. Once again, however, we must note that it is difficult to ascertain the degree of enforcement.

The first law concerning homosexual practices under the Christian emperors became effective in 342. In rather mocking terms it prohibited homosexual relations between men, on the pain of capital punishment. This law was rewritten about fifty years later in more serious language as an edict by the emperors Valentinian II, Theodosious, and Arcadius: "All persons who have the shameful custom of condemning a man's body, acting the part of a woman's . . . shall expiate this sort of crime in avenging flames."[19]

It was under the leadership of Emperor Justinian (527–565) that the scope of the law was extended to cover all kinds of homosexual activity. A series of natural disasters had ravaged the empire, and he saw this as the judgment of God for sin within his realm. Therefore, the laws against homosexuality in his famous revision of the Roman legal code published in 533 are phrased in terms of both personal disaster and social devastation: "We admonish men to abstain from the aforesaid unlawful acts, that they may not lose their souls . . . so that the city and the state may not come to harm by reason of such wicked deeds."[20]

While the imperial courts wrote and rewrote their laws, the church expressed its concerns in the context of canon law, that is, the legal system that developed within the church to maintain discipline in the community and to avoid the necessity of recourse to the government courts. The Council of Elvira (Spain) as early as 309 formulated a ruling against homosexual acts (canon 71). The rules of conduct circulated by Basil (see pp. 136-137) and other lists of rules composed in different areas of the church indicate that the written law of the church was always critical of homosexuality.

How did the establishment of such statutes affect the task of the Christian teachers? Did the laws solve the social problem? To some extent they did serve to make homosexual exploitation a less pressing issue, but it did not eradicate the concern. Therefore, the Fathers of the fourth and fifth centuries continued to speak out in clear terms against homosexual activity.

## John Chrysostom

John Chrysostom of Antioch (c. 347–407) was such a powerful preacher that even the name attributed to him by admirers attests his ability. Chrysostom in Greek means "golden mouth!" He is perhaps the best-known minister of early Christian history. Among the Greek fathers, no one has left so extensive and widely translated literary legacy. A large percentage of his writings are expository sermons in which he comments on the Bible and applies it to the situation in which he found himself. His bluntness and ardor for the truth that radiates from his sermons caused him much suffering and finally led him to a death in exile at the hands of corrupt imperial authorities who had been excited against him by jealous ecclesiastical colleagues. Professor Quasten has commented, "The tragedy of his life caused by his extraordinary sincerity and integrity of his character served but to enhance his glory and fame."[21]

His sermons on Romans were preached at Antioch before he was elected bishop. The collection constitutes the best early commentary on the epistle and is of enduring value. For his fourth sermon on this Pauline epistle, John chose as the text Romans 1:26–27 and proceeded to give an extended analysis of the problem of homosexuality. He observed that "all these affections [male and female homosexuality] were vile." To change one's sexual orientation or to accept the possibility of change is to change the creation of God and so change the truth of God to a lie. Whatever is contrary to God's created nature is a false pleasure. "For genuine pleasure is that which is according to nature." When people push God out of their lives, "not only is their doctrine satanical, but their life, too, is diabolical." This insult against nature undermines social stability and restricts personal joy. John Chrysostom argued that if they had sought pleasure according to nature, "they would have enjoyed it with more sense of security and greater joy, and so have been far removed from shameful deeds."[22]

This misplaced sexual interest is a result, primarily, of two factors. The first is the transgression of the law of God. The propensity toward sin in the other areas of one's life leads to a more general preoccupation with that which is unlawful. The second causative factor of misplaced sexual interest is that "the greater part of it came from their love of luxury, which also kindled into flame their lust."[23] They had "made a business of sin." Thus it happens, he argued, that society can become so confused and disoriented that people actually make an effort to become involved in sin.

Those who engage in any type of unlawful sexual behavior are to be pitied, Chrysostom said. They merit compassion because they become so involved in their unacceptable sexual patterns that they injure their own lives. This they do unknowingly, for they are blinded by their lust. They are unconscious of their plight. Life loses its proper orientation. Manhood becomes worthless. This aberrant behavior was a common concern of early Christian writers and applied also to lavish personal care, clothing, and other comforts.

Sexual sin in general, and homosexuality in particular, has both social and eternal ramifications. Chrysostom believed that the most pernicious of the social consequences was the strife between the sexes. He observed that homosexuality had a destructive effect on family life. It was not merely that he was concerned about the procreation of children. He was also concerned that people whose orientation is to their own sex will be in opposition to the divine declaration that the two "will become one flesh" (Gen. 2:24). The family structure so integral to the survival of society is endangered by sexual sin.

The judgment of God on this pattern of behavior is mirrored for all time, suggested Chrysostom, in the judgment of Sodom. This solemn warning interpreted for the church in Jude 7 is presented as a reminder of both possible present and certain future recompense. However, it is important in understanding Chrysostom's view as articulated in this sermon to note that the judgment of Sodom occurred not only because of the homosexual perversion present there. It was also because an entire society's values and concerns had become warped. The abomination of homosexual activity is no less abominable than the behavior that tolerates the admiration of the rich for the sake of their riches and always seeks additional comfort and luxury.

He then returns to his central theme:

> You have made the race dishonored through irrational behavior, by such indignities toward yourselves and one another. From where did these evils arise? Of luxury; of not knowing God. For so soon as any have cast out fear of Him, all that is good straightway goes to ruin.[24]

Instead of seeking that which leads to estrangement from God and involvement in sin, urges Chrysostom, seek the true wealth and true pleasure:

> Take up virtue and the pleasure which comes thereof. For so both here and hereafter shall we come to enjoy great delights and shall attain the promised blessings through the grace and goodness toward mankind of our Lord Jesus Christ.[25]

The focus, then, of Chrysostom's critique of homosexuality is twofold. First, homosexuality is the symptom of a deeper malaise within society. If man is right in social and spiritual relationships, the assumption is that there would be no problem of misplaced sexual orientation. If, however, the theological views of society are inadequate, if values develop a this-worldly emphasis, and if persons are valued for their riches or physical attractiveness, then homosexual behavior and other sexual practices regarded as sinful are certain to result.

Chrysostom's second point concerning homosexuality is that the person who is a victim of the society in which he or she must live and who in turn accelerates the decadence of that society is to be the object of Christian pity and remedial effort. At the same time, he objected in no uncertain terms to toleration of homosexuality or other sexual sins within the church because of their tendency to corrupt personal morality.

Chrysostom often returned to this theme of the relationship

between society and sin. He juxtaposed the evident causal nexus of the two with the position of a Christian who has the divinely ordained obligation to serve as a redemptive force in love, not compromising the biblical commandments. Christians are to adhere to sound doctrine, he said. They are to strive for Christian perfection. They are not to be legalists but are to go beyond the law, seeking "the things of God which are enduring and are above all change or end. For the glory of that state is not from without but from within."[26]

### Augustine

In the vast literature that came from the prolific pen of Augustine (354–430), the spirited bishop of Hippo in North Africa, are three sermons in which he deals with the problem of sexual sin. He takes as his text for the first sermon the words of Paul in 1 Corinthians 6: "Do not be deceived: Neither the sexually immoral nor idolaters nor adulterers nor male prostitutes nor homosexual offenders ... will inherit the kingdom of God.... Do you not know that your bodies are members of Christ?" (vv. 9–10, 15). These two foci—that sinners do not possess the kingdom of God and that the bodies of believers are the members of Christ—were kept continually before the audience. Augustine reasoned that since the Christian's body is "a temple of the Holy Spirit" (v. 19), the Christian has an obligation to keep his person as pure as possible. Only the individual who maintains a distance from sinful habits has the privilege of entering the kingdom of God. Those who do not keep themselves pure are excluded, "For there will be a New Heaven and a New Earth which the righteous shall inhabit. There the ungodly, there the wicked, there the abandoned are not allowed to dwell."[27] Those whose life styles place them within the context of the list of sins in 1 Corinthians 6:9–11 have the possibility of changing their way, by the grace of God. Those who do not avail themselves of this opportunity will be judged severely.

The second sermon in this series delves more deeply into the psychological ramifications of the problem as Augustine understood them. Here his primary concern is fornication, but he makes it clear throughout that the same critique applies to all the activities listed in the 1 Corinthians passage. Each of these are "sins of violence and impurity." As persons become involved in the great abomination of fornication or homosexuality, they "cannot think or attend to anything else."[28] That individual eventually becomes a captive of violence, lust, and carnality. He or she becomes a slave to the body. This preoccupation drives out the proper reason for being—that is, to function as the temple of the Spirit of God. When this temple is defiled by sin, it is abandoned by God, and mankind is left to his unworthy preoccupations.

Augustine's solution to sin in the lives of those who wish to be Christian is presented in the final sermon. Taking as his text, Galatians 5:16, "Live by the Spirit, and you will not gratify the desires of the sinful nature," he proposes that victory over the sins listed in 1 Corinthians 6:9–11 is possible. It is not by law that "these are to be as idols broken down in us."[29] Law makes our situation worse. It is by grace given by God and by our own determination to restore the temple of the Spirit of God that security is achieved. Augustine recognized that the process of restoration is arduous and that it often seems a hopeless goal. But victory is possible: "Let us believe, hope, love; someday there will be victory."

He closes this sermon of exhortation and hope by saying:

> Therefore when you have begun to labor in your struggle against the lusts of the flesh, walk in the Spirit, invoke the Spirit, seek the gift of God. And if the law of your members (that is, your habits) resist the law of your mind from your inferior part, that is the flesh, and hold you captive under the law of sin, this too shall be rectified. This too shall pass over into the rights of victory. . . . If you (acknowledge your weakness) believing, humbly . . . the answer is made, the Grace of God through Jesus Christ our Lord.[30]

Augustine and Chrysostom are but two of a great number of influential writers who addressed this issue through the medium of preaching.

## Basil

The same method was employed by Basil (330–379), bishop of Caesarea in Cappadocia. He became known as Basil the Great because of his vigorous efforts in defense of orthodoxy and in service to the poor and outcast both locally and in the intrigue-filled provincial and national capitals. The son of a wealthy nobleman, Basil gave away his entire fortune so that he could more effectively devote himself to ministry. The lack of possessions and dwellings rendered him immune to the threats of his enemies, enabling him to follow his conscience and the leading of the Spirit of God with such firmness and courage that the emperor ceased attempting to drive him to submission or into exile. Such was the extraordinary moral and spiritual stature of Basil.

Among Basil's voluminous writings is a sermon entitled "God Is Not the Author of Evil." Here he argues on the basis of Psalm 14:1–2 that he who says, either by word or through his actions, "There is no God," becomes corrupt and does abominable deeds. These people surrender, are given over, to unworthy passions. One of these reprehensible activities is homosexuality. This is an "ignominius life style" which "changes the natural processes into those which are unnatural."[31] This in turn reduces the glory of God in man to the level of the animals. It is not to this end that man was created in the image of God. The acts of God and of those devoted to Him are to be in harmony with nature and with the concerns of the gospel.

Basil's emphatic rejection of homosexuality within the context of the Christian community is also evident from a letter to Amphilochius, bishop of Iconium. This letter is the third in a series of letters articulating regulations for Christian communities attempting to maintain order in a period of social instability. Each rule is accompanied by instructions for disciplining offenders within the legal system of the church. Rule number 72 states, "He who commits an indecency with men is to be disciplined for a period of time [equivalent] to one who has transgressed in adultery."[32]

This rule, as well as the others, became the standard expression of the prescriptions for ecclesiastical discipline throughout the Greek-speaking church. Why should purity be maintained within the church? Those who sin and refuse to abandon their sinful habits serve their own desires instead of Christ. All Christians, ever mindful of present and future judgment, must avoid being ensnared in the evil perpetrated by the impious and they have the responsibility of offering a clear indication to the impious of the way to salvation.

The literary production from this period was of such quality and quantity that this era has been called the golden age of Greek patristic literature. It is from this time that the first great systematic biblical commentaries have been preserved. The normal method was to begin at verse one of chapter one of a given book of the Bible and proceed to the end. Nearly every phrase was quoted and then followed by a few words or several paragraphs of explanation. These brief statements tell us what the authors thought the texts meant and often hint at an application to the practical issues confronting the Fathers and the church of their day. In their writings we find the most basic instruction offered to the church by its greatest teachers, who sought to instruct the community in the art of interpreting the Bible.

We will consider four of the commentators. Pelagius and "Ambrosiaster" are two of the most important commentators of the Latin-speaking church of the fourth and fifth centuries. Theodore of Mopsuestia and Theodoret are perhaps the most significant from the Greek-speaking church.

## Pelagius

Pelagius, the great antagonist of Augustine, commented on each of the Pauline epistles. His observations, written between 406 and 409, are laconic, precise, and usually a careful, accurate elaboration of Paul's own words. Awareness of the work of his predecessors on the Pauline corpus is evident. There is nothing of the acrimony of the later debates. Throughout his commentaries, whenever the text allows, he champions the principle that persons are judged eternally for their works as well as for their faith. This is the case in each of the Pauline references to homosexuality. On Romans 1:26–27 he quotes the apocryphal Wisdom of Solomon: "The worship of idols without actual existence is the beginning, the cause and the end of all evil" (14:27). Here he argues, as did the authors before him, that each of these actions indicate disoriented theological values. The consequences of such values is offered in a comment on 1 Corinthians 6:9–10: "Do not be mistaken, thinking that faith alone is sufficient for salvation."[33] All who become entwined by sin are excluded from the kingdom of God. This is for him, as well, a conclusive argument that mankind does not have a fixed nature. If we are indeed responsible for our behavior, we have the potential to determine the ethic by which we live. Then, in commenting on 1 Timothy 1:9–10, he exhorts the reader to avoid the unnatural and that which is against the doctrines of the gospel.

### Ambrosiaster

The name of perhaps the most important early Latin commentator is unknown to us. He is called Ambrosiaster for his works were preserved under the name of another man, that is, Ambrose, bishop of Milan. (The suffix -aster means "inferior," "not genuine.") Written between 366 and 384, this is the first attempt to provide a commentary on the epistles of Paul that in itself comprised a literary unit. This author offered observations on each of the Pauline sin lists. In writing on these and other passages, he develops his understanding of sin, the law, repentance, and the Christian lifestyle.

Natural righteousness, he said, is possible for those whose behavior is consonant with what is inherently right. This, however, provides only a "temporal righteousness." Faith in Christ is necessary for "eternal righteousness." This does not mean that the Christian is free from moral obligations. Quite the contrary. The person who believes has no fear of the judgment before God with respect to faith. However, for every Christian there is a judgment for his life and life style. In this respect, all of the sins listed in Romans 1:26–27, 1 Corinthians 6:9–11, and 1 Timothy 1:9–10 are equally grievous and serious.

Ambrosiaster regarded homosexuality as a form of idolatry. Those who would express their sexuality in a way "contrary to nature" are usurping the place of the Creator. Satan also had tried to take the place of God, and as was Satan, so the human usurpers will be excluded from the kingdom of God.

This Christian responsibility for righteous living is not to be confused with living under the law. With Paul, Ambrosiaster argues that "those who have accepted remission of sins do not live under the law, but are liberated by a gift of God through faith in Christ."[34] The new life is not regulated by a law written in detail. It is a life lived out in contemplation of the gospel of Christ and application thereof to the daily existence; it is a life lived in harmony with the nature that God created.

## Theodore of Mopsuestia

Theodore of Mopsuestia (c. 350–428), a close friend of John Chrysostom, was a careful scholar and biblical exegete with a reputation for erudition and orthodoxy, though his orthodoxy would be challenged by future generations. His one goal was to mediate the teaching of Paul to his era. Grateful readers, in recognition of his contribution, called him the "Interpreter."

Fundamental to Theodore's theological understanding is the distinction between the present state of sin and death and the future state of sinlessness and immortality. Christians have the promise of the glorious future after accepting faith and baptism. The glorious state is not yet perfectly realized in their earthly life, but in this life it is potentially there and must be nurtured by their best efforts. Christians are to strive to live in harmony with the ideals of resurrection life. This involves abstention from those activities, including homosexuality, that are listed in 1 Timothy 1:9–10. (Unfortunately, his comments on Romans 1:26–27 and 1 Corinthians 6:9–11 have been lost.)

139

Those whose lives are characterized by participation in sin (anything not in accordance with the gospel of God) have been provided here with a law that is corrective and remedial. The restoration to harmony with nature and God is accomplished in the birth, death, and resurrection of Jesus Christ. Through the operation of the Holy Spirit, the Christian is given the possibility and responsibility of molding the present existence into a model of the future life.

### Theodoret

Theodoret (c. 393–c. 458) served as bishop of Cyrrhus, a small town near Antioch in Syria. He was widely recognized by his contemporaries as a masterful scholar and theologian. He also was renowned for his active and eminently practical concern for both the spiritual and the temporal welfare of his parishioners. He addressed the problem of homosexuality in his commentaries and in a written defense of Christianity against paganism.

In his commentaries on the biblical text, he observes that "major and minor sins" should cause the unrepentant to despair of salvation (on 1 Cor. 6:9–11). All of these sins, including homosexuality, change the truth of God to untruth and change legitimate desires into expressions of impiety (on Rom. 1:26–27). These patterns of behavior, he observes, were prohibited by the Old Testament law. "But these also we ourselves, the proclaimers of the New Testament, prohibit." He continues, using the words of Paul to express his ideal: "We prohibit . . . whatever else is contrary to sound doctrine, in accordance with the glorious gospel of the blessed God with which I have been entrusted" (cf. 1 Tim. 1:10–11).[35]

Even as bishop of a town near where centuries before the followers of Christ were first called Christians, Theodoret found that many people still believed the fables about the Greek gods. His response to this, entitled *The Cure of Pagan Maladies or The Truth of the Gospels Proved From Greek Philosophy*, has been recognized as the best existing refutation of paganism.

In this work he deals with the major and age-old questions of religion, philosophy, and ethics, showing the superiority of Christianity to the alternatives. In the context of a discussion of "the laws," he notes that Plato had condoned homosexual practice. This, he argues, is not compatible with the value that Christians place on marriage. Marriage, for the Christian, is to be an indissoluble union in accord with the exhortations of the Gospels and of the apostles. Any behavior deleterious to the sanctity of marriage is to be avoided by Christians.

Later, in a chapter on "Angels, Gods and Demons," Theodoret declares that in pagan theology the angels and gods are, in effect, victims of intemperance and "slaves of homosexuality." This theology, he argues, does not correspond to what we know about nature and divinity. He urges the readers to examine the various pagan and Christian alternatives and to "judge which of these two conceptions best match the invisible realities."[36] He did not doubt that the Christian understanding of the nature of angels and of God more adequately describes reality.

## Concluding Observations

This survey of the view of homosexuality in the writings of the church fathers does not pretend to be a complete catalog of references to and discussions of the issue during the first five centuries of the Christian era. Only a few of the works of the most important authors have been analyzed here.

These authors, as we have noted, usually discussed the problem of homosexuality with reference to the lists of sins in Paul's epistles. Their literal approach to the ethics section of the New Testament left them with no doubt that homosexuality in all of its manifestations was condemned by God. However, the problem was rarely singled out and addressed alone. The Fathers insisted that all the sins listed by Paul were equally serious and each would exclude the sinner from the kingdom of God.

In seeking to apply the sin lists to the problems confronting the church, the Fathers appropriated them to explain what it means to be a disciple of Christ. These early leaders of the church argued that Christians were intended to be a people set apart. As the people of God, they were to avoid all forms of interpersonal exploitation, to contend for social justice and righteousness, and to live in harmony with nature. All of the actions listed in Romans 1:26–27; 1 Corinthians 6:9–11; and 1 Timothy 1:9–10 were condemned as being diametrically opposed to social and personal well-being and fraught with consequences beyond the limits of this life.

Sex and marriage were always important issues in the definition of what it meant to be Christian. Over the centuries the debate concerning the purpose of sex and marriage continued. The varying views ranged from absolute abstinence from sexual relationships to what we would consider a "healthy" view of sex and family life. The great majority of the Fathers contended for the sanctity of marriage within the Christian community. They insisted that marriage be monogamous and that the relationship must not be dissolved.

They were unanimous in condemning homosexuality, adultery, fornication, bestiality, and greed—all of which were viewed as symptomatic expressions of the distorted values and interpersonal relationships in the non-Christian social matrix.

For these writers, sexual and social sin was a negation of the image of God in man, making impossible the restoration of that image by the indwelling Spirit of God. The person who had accepted the Christian faith had the responsibility to strive toward Christian perfection, living a life consistent with the ethic of the Christian community as defined in the Gospels and the Pauline epistles. The work of Jesus Christ made freedom from sin possible, and it was the duty of every Christian to progress toward the actualization of that possibility.

Certainly, the emphatic nature of their statements were provoked and conditioned by the excesses that the Fathers observed in Greco-Roman society, as well as by their conviction that the pagan theologies that permitted and encouraged such behavior were inadequate as guides for life in this world or in the next. The early writers, in conformity with the Pauline model, insisted that Christians should have no part in these sins and that those who did thus sin would be excluded from the kingdom of God.

The new people of God were to be a redemptive influence in society as a whole as well as for the individual in that society. One prerequisite for those who would serve as leaven in their world is abstention from the sins cataloged in the Pauline sin lists.

Today, the task of the Christian is the same as that of our forerunners in the faith. The believer must answer the question, What does it mean to be His disciple? The relevant issues must be analyzed and defined from a Christian and social heritage. Then the implications of that analysis must be fearlessly carried out in faith.

This survey of the Fathers of the Christian church deals with only a selected few of the great teachers of the church. For further reading in the sources themselves, consult Johannes Quasten's *Patrology*.[37] This work provides an excellent, concise introduction to each author and a list of texts and translations of each work. The abbreviated references are included in this chapter so that the readers may verify the work cited or quoted for themselves or, if they wish, examine the context more closely.

# 4

# Biology, Psychology, and Homosexuality

The author is Professor of Psychiatry, Head of the Division of Biological Psychiatry, and Head of the Division of Electroencephalography at Duke University Medical Center, Durham, North Carolina. He is a graduate of Duke University, B.S., and Duke University School of Medicine, M.D., and is a Research Fellow in Medicine in the Department of Psychiatry and Medicine at Duke Medical School, a Resident in Psychiatry at Duke Medical School, and a Fellow in EEG, Montreal Neurological Institute in Montreal, Canada. Dr. Wilson has had over one hundred forty scientific articles published and is a member of several medical and psychiatric organizations. He is president of The United Methodist Renewal Services Fellowship of Nashville, Tennessee, and a member of the Board of Directors of the Good News Movement within the United Methodist Church, Wilmore, Kentucky.

## By William P. Wilson

# Homosexuality

in the Old Testament
in the New Testament
in church history
**in the physical and emotional**
in the courtroom
in the church

**4** Normal males and normal females are unmistakably different. They differ from each other physically, endocrinologically, physiologically, psychologically, and behaviorally. "Biological intent is to differentiate males and females ... in such a manner as to insure species survival which can be served only through heterosexual union."[1] God, as the author of nature, designed man and woman as companions whose complementariness would provide an appropriate environment in which new beings could be raised to maturity and thus continue the species. Homosexuality is, therefore, a deviation from the normal and as such has been the subject of attention throughout recorded history.

With the development of modern science, the early investigators of homosexuality considered it to have its origin in the physical workings of the body. Both Krafft-Ebing and Havelock-Ellis believed that it had a constitutional, or hereditary, cause.[2] With the development of Freudian dynamic psychiatry, there was an abrupt swing away from this position to one that emphasized early-life experiences as being the primary cause. W. J. Gadpaille has noted that there are two distinct theoretical positions—biological and environmental. According to the first theory, there is an innate biological sexuality and a child's development proceeds through a series of phases representing partial instincts that must ultimately become integrated harmoniously for adult sexual functioning. Some of the phases will be more difficult than others for the child to complete successfully, depending in large part on his constitutional make-up. The second theory, emphasizing environment, finds "a typical family constellation in the background of male homosexuals, consisting of a close binding intimate mother and a detached, indifferent or hostile father. The mother's influence demasculinized the son and stripped the father of admirable masculine qualities, and the father made identification with himself unpalatable."[3] It is this latter theoretical model that has gained the most support from studies of both male and female homosexuals.

For those who accept the second theory, there remains, however, the problem that it is most difficult to change the sexual orientation of the homosexual. Equally difficult to change are the behavioral variations observed in some of these individuals.[4] These behavioral differences are so profound that even though one is convinced that homosexuality has its origin in early-life experiences one may nevertheless suspect that in time a cause will be found in the inner workings of the body. Reinforcing this doubt are animal studies that have suggested that the brain not only determines the endocrinal differences found in the two sexes,[5] but also controls to some degree the behavioral differences.[6] It is, therefore, impossible to ignore research that has investigated the genetic and hormonal aspects of both normal and abnormal human sexual behavior.

### BIOLOGICAL ASPECTS

*Differentiation of Normal Sexual Behavior*

Corinne Hutt has surveyed the literature relating to early-life development in behavior of males and females.[7] She noted that some authors had stated that boys and girls were the same at birth and that they adjusted to their sex assignment irrespective of their hormonal or genetic sex.[8] This idea was advanced because hermaphrodites (persons whose external sexual apparatus is not consistent with their sex-hormone-secreting glands), who were often anatomically masculinized females or feminized males, did adopt the attitudes, opinions, dress, and mannerisms of their assigned sex. This, however, is not the same as *role adoption*,[9] which relates to observable sex-related behaviors such as activity levels, exploratory behavior, and nurturing attentiveness. Biological factors should affect the latter especially in the homosexual. It is because of the interrelatedness of role identification, role adoption, and sexual object choice that one must study the differentiation of normal sexual behavior in early life as a basis for understanding anomalies, that is, deviations from the normal.

It is not within the scope of this chapter to review in detail the sexual differentiation of the developing unborn child (fetus). It is, however, important to mention a few significant facts about this differentiation. The first of these relates to the importance of the Y (male) chromosome (see explanation on page 152) in the determination of maleness. The Y chromosome results in differentiation as a male except when the cells in the body of the developing child are insensitive to male sex hormone. This is true even when there is one or more extra X (female) chromosomes. Once the fetal male sex glands (testes) are formed, they secrete testosterone, a male hormone that causes the development of male sex organs (genitalia). As the fetus develops, this same male sex hormone (testosterone) also causes a differentiation of the brain into that of a male. This differentiation, necessary because the control of hormone secretion in the female is cyclic whereas that of the male is acyclic, takes place in an area in the base of the brain called the hypothalamus. The hypothalamus controls the secretion of hormones from the pituitary gland that in turn control the secretion of hormones by all other glands in the body including the ovaries and testes. Two areas of the hypothalamus control the secretion of these hormones. One area governs a tonic, or continuous, secretion. The other governs a cyclic or periodic secretion. It is this latter area of the hypothalamus, called the preoptic, that is larger in the female.[10] The hypothalamus is also an area that in part controls drives and emotional behavior.

With continuing development, there is further physical differentiation.[11] At birth males exceed females in both weight and length. Males have a higher metabolic rate and a higher caloric intake. Males are slightly more active than females in total motor activity. Their motor behavior is also quite different in that male activity consists of grosser movements.

Studies of mother-infant interaction reveal a significant difference between males and females in interaction with their mothers. Male infants are more irritable than females, and there is, therefore, significantly more interaction. However, this seems to be less true at older ages, though mothers continue to stimulate male children more. It is important to realize that interactional differences seem to be the outcome of behavior that is occurring because of the sex of the child.

As children grow older, obvious sex-related differences in behavior continue. Males are less reluctant to leave their mothers and are less fearful. They are more likely to seek solutions to problems. Males are more aggressive, both displaying and eliciting more aggression. Acquisitive competition also is stronger among males. Aggressive behavior appears to be related to the presence of male sex hormone early in the development of the child before birth.

Females display increased aggressive behavior when they are exposed to hormones that are masculinizing in the womb because of a defect in cortisone (a hormone from the adrenal glands) or when large doses of progestin (a female hormone that has some masculinizing effects) are given to prevent a miscarriage. In contrast to observations of increased aggressive behavior in males are the observations that cooperation is a far more feminine trait. Most studies have demonstrated that females display a remarkable degree of maternalistic or nurturing attentiveness early in life. There is also a great tendency for males and females to interact predominately with members of their own sex.

Males are far more exploratory than females and are considered to be more creative. Whether this is related to intelligence differences is not clear, but the data demonstrate that, where reasoning or the logical manipulation of concepts or relationships is concerned, males are superior, irrespective of the content of the problem. This is true whether the content is expressed in numbers, words, or patterns.

In concluding her summary of sex differentiation in the human, Hutt makes the point that "genetic complements confer special properties on the course of development, but gonadal hormones and the testicular hormones in particular have important formative and organizational functions. From the moment of birth onwards, differences in structures, in metabolism, in physiological, in psychological functions characterize the development of the two sexes." She concludes by stating that the sex-related developmental similarities between monkeys, chimpanzees, and children make a purely environmental interpretation of "normal" sex differences difficult to accept.[12]

*Genetics*

In the reproductive cells of every species of animal there is material carrying information that determines the appearance, life functions, and to some extent the behavior of every member of that species. This material will divide at certain stages of the development of the cell into bits that are called chromosomes. Each of these chromosomes is made up of many smaller bits. These are called genes. Each reproductive cell—that of the male (called sperm) and that of the female (called ovum)—carries one half of the material necessary to form a complete cell that will develop into an adult individual. Because there are many divisions that occur in the development of the reproductive cells, errors can occur. Sometimes divisions will take place that leave the developing sperm or ovum with too many or too few chromosomes of a particular kind. When any of these cells are involved in reproduction, the individual is born with an abnormal number of chromosomes. Most of the time, however, this abnormality (in nonsex chromosomes) causes the death of the cell. If sex chromosomes are too many or too few, the cell does not die. Excesses or deficiencies of some other chromosomes may produce abnormalities affecting other organ systems.

Some diseases have their origin in the organization of the building blocks of genes. These abnormalities are not lethal but instead give rise to such diseases as high blood pressure, diabetes, certain kinds of epilepsy, and many other diseases. It is believed that some behavior is in part determined by the structure of genes.

In the light of the evidence that sexual behavior in normal humans seems to some extent genetically determined, what evidence is there to suggest that homosexuality may be of genetic origin? The obvious place to begin is in the examination of the data found in reports of studies of genetic transmission of homosexuality or the occurrence of this condition in persons with genetic abnormalities.

F. J. Kallman's report that homosexuality in forty identical twin pairs affected both of the twins similarly has never been refuted or confirmed.[13] There are, however, a number of criticisms of his study. The first is that there should have been a high incidence of homosexuality among the fathers of the homosexual twins. There was not! Second, the majority of the twins were mentally ill with a disease called schizophrenia or they had severe personality problems. The fact that they were mentally ill distorts the patient population. Third, each pair of twins was reared together. This suggests that environmentally determined factors could have been just as important as their genetic similarity. Therefore, it is unwise to draw any conclusions from Kallman's data!

Studies of persons with abnormal numbers of chromosomes shed light on the determination of sexual behavior.[14] Klinefelter's syndrome, a condition in which there is an extra female chromosome in a male (XXY) (two female chromosomes and one male chromosome), has an increased incidence of homosexuality and transvestism (dressing in clothes of the opposite sex). Individuals with this syndrome are anatomically male, but their genitalia may not enlarge at puberty and their body build may be eunuchoid (female), with breast development. Their testes are usually small and do not produce sperm. Their sex drive is low, and sexual activity, if it occurs, is infrequent.

The XYY syndrome, a condition in which there is an extra male chromosome, was initially thought to be always characterized by impulsiveness, aggression, and violence. Although subsequent research has only in part corroborated these observations, not all cases manifest these traits. Homosexuality may also occur in the XYY syndrome.

Turner's syndrome is a condition characterized by an absence of the normal complement of sex chromosomes (XO). In individuals with this abnormality the internal reproductive structures do not form, even though the external genitalia are female. In the absence of ovaries, puberty does not take place. Even so, these individuals are characteristically female. Interestingly, on psychological tests that differentiate masculine from feminine interests females with Turner's syndrome have greater feminine interests than normal women. They are not reported to be homosexual.

In summary, it cannot be demonstrated that homosexual behavior is directly produced by the transmission of genetically determined behavior or by the occurrence of an excessive or deficient number of sex chromosomes. It is true that extra female or male chromosomes influence sexual behavior, but this does not necessarily mean they cause homosexuality. It may be speculated that in Klinefelter's syndrome the extra X chromosome interferes in some way with the normal organization of the brain in determining sexual behavior. This gives rise to the decreased sex drive that is common in this problem. In the XYY syndrome the organization of the brain may be changed so as to result in increased aggression. In the XO syndrome the absence of sex hormones, arising from a failure of the ovaries to develop, gives rise to brain development that results in increased feminine behavior. It is possible that the changes in Klinefelter's syndrome (XXY) and Turner's syndrome (XO) are entirely related to the hormonal deficiencies and are secondary to the genetic defects. The occurrence of homosexuality in Klinefelter's and the XYY syndromes cannot be considered to be related to the genetic defect or to hormonal changes since it is infrequent.

## Hormonal

There are two major biological differences between men and women. These are (1) the secretion of different sex hormones and (2) the cyclic secretory processes of the female sex hormones. It is conceivable, at least biologically, that some abnormality of hormonal secretion at some time in the homosexual's development might cause his condition.

Animal behavior is profoundly influenced by the presence of androgens (hormones that have masculinizing properties) not only at critical times in the development of the fetus but also throughout life. It has been suggested that nature's prime purpose in reproduction is to produce females. Maleness results only from the effects of androgens. In the absence of androgens or androgen effects, whether the fetus is female (XX) or male (XY), the anatomical development and behavior of the individual will be female.

In the presence of androgens, the development and behavior will be male. Even small quantities of androgens at appropriate times in the life of the fetus of an animal will cause the brain to develop so that the infant and adult animal will display behavior that is considered masculine. Human females may be masculinized as a result of a defect in cortisone metabolism. This defect produces large quantities of androgens, which in turn cause the external sexual organs to appear masculine and produce a decided tendency toward masculine behavior. This tendency occurs whether the genital defect is corrected early or late. This phenomenon is interpreted as indicating a direct relationship between the presence of the androgens and masculine behavior. Females who have this condition exhibit increased homosexual activity and inclination and respond with increased arousal to visual and narrative stimuli. This same observation has been made of women who had hermaphroditism induced by progestin.

In contrast, there are males who have what is called the androgen insensitivity syndrome. These males are born with a normal genetic compliment (XY), but because of an inherited defect in enzymes, the tissues of the developing unborn child do not respond to secreted testosterone, and the individuals who are genetic males are born as perfectly normal-looking girls. They are reared as girls, and their condition is discovered only when they fail to menstruate. Investigation usually reveals that they are actually male (XY). The gender identity, assignment, and rearing has, however, been unequivocally feminine. These individuals function quite well as female when appropriate surgery and hormonal administration is carried out. Gadpaille comments that "nature will differentiate a female in the absence of effective fetal androgen and that chromosomal hormonal and gonadal sex is regularly overriden by this female first principle and by gender of assignment and rearing."[15]

The evidence presented in this section makes it clear that hormones play a critical role in the development of the external genitalia and in the future determination of sexual behavior. The most critical time is in the first few months after conception, for it is during that time that the development of the testes and ovaries takes place. The presence of testes influences the development of male external genitalia and this in turn determines gender assignment and rearing. Both factors are inseparably linked so that hormonal disturbances in fetal life affect both the structure of the genitals and sexual behavior in later life. It is this knowledge that is of critical importance as we now evaluate the data obtained in studies of homosexuals.

## Studies of Homosexuals

During the past few years, a number of studies have been conducted in an effort to determine whether there may be a biological basis for homosexuality. In our foregoing discussion of sexual behavior, we have noted that there is little evidence to support the notion that homosexuality is solely a genetically transmissable behavior. Neither genetic studies of identical twins nor studies of genetic abnormalities support this possibility. Evidence does, however, support the consideration that hormonal disturbances could be the cause. The two periods of development when hormonal influences would be most likely to affect behavior would be during the period of developmental organization of the hypothalamic nuclei before birth and in the remainder of the period of growth prior to puberty. In this latter instance, the period immediately after birth is a time of greatest vulnerability.

We have noted previously that if the organization of the hypothalamus is female, it could cause homosexuality in the male. If this is so, then it should be possible to demonstrate a cyclic, female type of gonadotropic secretion. Gonadotropins are the pituitary hormones that control the secretion of the male and female sex hormones. This pattern of secretion would result from the failure of the testes to secrete adequate quantities of testosterone during the prenatal period. One could then explain the homosexual's role adoption and sexual-object choice by the hypothalamic misdevelopment that also gave rise to female gonadotropin release patterns. However, this is not the case. Although the studies conducted by Halbreich and others do reveal significant day-to-day variations from normal, the average secretion rate was the same for homosexuals as for heterosexuals. There was no significant evidence of cyclic variation. The increased variation in daily secretion was, however, thought possibly to be due to a deficiency of testosterone in the perinatal period, that is, around the time of birth.[16] Careful inspection of the data of these authors, however, does not lead one to believe that the patterns of secretion could be considered typically female. The earlier work of Doerr, Kolodny, and others did not clarify this issue either.[17]

The second possibility (that there is deficient testosterone secretion after birth) is also not consistently borne out by a number of investigators. Loraine, Kolodny, and their associates did report lowered levels of plasma testosterone and a high incidence of azoospermia (inability to produce spermatozoa) in male homosexuals. They postulated that these findings might be compatible with a possible biological predisposition to homosexuality.[18] Migeon had been unable to find a consistent pattern of lowered testosterone levels and in one instance found a high level.[19] More recently, Starka and others have been able to demonstrate significantly lower levels of testosterone in males who had normal levels of plasma testosterone.[20] Other authors have found no consistent differences.[21]

These studies do not explain the relationships of gonado-tropin and testosterone secretion to homosexuality. The inconsistent variations in gonadotropin secretions may be due to the absence of ovaries to respond to a cyclic release. On the other hand, the low testosterone levels in adult life may indicate an earlier deficiency that influenced the development of feminine behavior when the hypothalamic nuclei were not sufficiently stimulated to develop the male brain structure. The fact that some normal males and homosexuals can have a similar gonadotropin release and similar low levels of testosterone would not lead one to believe that these hormonal disturbances have caused males to be homosexual.

Physiological differences in homosexual males have seldom been reported. Zung and Wilson, who studied arousal from sleep, noted that normal females are significantly more arousable from sleep by auditory stimuli than are normal males in all stages of sleep except that of Rapid Eye Movement (REM).[22] Wilson and his coauthors compared the arousability of homosexual males to that of normal males and females and found that there was a significant similarity of arousability of homosexuals to that of females. There was a significant difference in the arousability from sleep of normal and homosexual males in the second, third, and fourth stages of sleep.[23] There are no other studies in which physiological responses of normal and homosexual males have been compared.

Masters and Johnson have reported no differences in the sexual physiology of homosexual males or females and that of their heterosexual brothers and sisters.[24]

Biologically determined behavioral differences that distinguish normal boys from normal girls have been mentioned earlier. Gadpaille quotes Money as saying that there are biologically determined behavioral differences that distinguish normal boys from normal girls. These are (1) a higher energy expenditure in males; (2) differences of preferences in play, toys, and sports; (3) boys' preferences for shirts, trousers, jeans, etc.;

(4) lack of maternalism in boys; (5) differences in career ambitions; (6) body image consonant with gender orientation; and (7) visual and narrative perceptual erotic arousal patterns in males.[25] There is, however, little evidence to support all of Money's assertions. It is true that boys seem more active in the first few months of life, play more aggressively, and are not maternalistic, but there are no data to suggest that dress and career ambitions are not entirely determined by the culture. Recent evidence refutes the notion that men and women differ in perceptual erotic arousal.[26] There are no data to support or refute the other assertions in his statement.

If we now ask what evidence there is to suggest that homosexual males may differ from normal males, we find that there is none. The only evidence we have supports the notion that homosexuals are biologically more like boys, since they are not maternalistic. In the light of this knowledge, then, it is not possible to say that homosexual boys have biologically determined behavior that is similar to that of girls.

An added bit of evidence that the basic masculine behavioral patterns are preserved in the male homosexual is the observation that he is similar in his search for sexual contacts to the less-inhibited heterosexual male. He tends to seek sex for sexual release and does not usually form long-lasting relationships as do lesbians, whose capacity for such relationships is similar to that of heterosexual women.[27]

To conclude this discussion of the biological basis for homosexuality, we must comment that medical treatments of homosexuality have not altered the object choice of the homosexual. Even though drugs and electric shock treatments have been given to these individuals usually for other psychiatric problems, there is no change of object choice even when the complicating disease has been successfully treated. This is in contrast to psychological treatments that are usually quite successful.[28] Such success is more evidence against a biological origin of the disease, for biologically determined mental disease is notoriously resistant to psychological intervention.

## PSYCHOLOGICAL ASPECTS

It is not possible to discuss in detail the psychological origins of homosexuality. Standard textbooks of psychiatry provide excellent summaries of the process by which the sexual-object choice becomes a person of the same sex. Most commonly it is, as we have mentioned earlier, the influence of a close, binding, intimate mother and a detached, indifferent, or hostile father who provide the appropriate stimuli to cause the child to identify himself sexually with the parent of the opposite sex. In some cases the child is dressed in clothes and encouraged in activities that are inappropriate. Other factors also contribute to the psychological origins of homosexuality. The reader is, however, referred to Socarides's or Bieber's books for details.[29]

### Psychological Studies

The American Psychiatric Association has removed the diagnosis of homosexuality from the *Diagnostic and Statistical Manual of Mental Disorders*. This decision was a result of a vote of the members of the organization. It is not likely that those voting made a decision based on new scientific evidence, for there was none. It is more likely that the vote reflects the extraordinary resistance of homosexuality to psychiatric intervention and the knowledge that most homosexuals live lives that are relatively free of conflict and symptoms. This statement is supported by the study of Weinberg and Williams in which they ascertained that 68 percent of homosexuals had never received treatment for their homosexuality and 82 percent had no desire for treatment. Most homosexuals, according to this study, saw themselves as persons of worth and were satisfied with themselves. They had a consistently good opinion of themselves. They rarely got depressed. But there was also an increased incidence of psychosomatic problems. They tended to suffer from insomnia, anorexia, anxiety, headache, gastrointestinal upset, and tremulousness. They often had nightmares and tended to misuse alcohol. In their interpersonal relationships, there was a sizable group who seemed to be introverted, but about 60 percent of them felt quite good about their interpersonal relationships. Their "faith in others" seemed to indicate a high degree of trust. These data were obtained by questionnaires from a large group of homosexuals who lived in a large urban area and who were not receiving psychiatric treatment.[30]

The intelligence of homosexuals is slightly above normal according to the studies of Raboch and Sipova.[31] Their data demonstrated a statistically significant artifact since there was a gross disparity in the size of their normal group and the sexually deviant groups.

More formal psychological examination of homosexuals has revealed little evidence of psychopathology. In 1957 Grygier summarized the literature and attempted to analyze the efficacy of the tests administered in determining the feminine orientation of some homosexuals.[32] In general, tests such as the Minnesota Multiphasic Personality Inventory (MMPI), the California Personality Inventory, and the Guilford-Martin Inventory of factors failed to differentiate homosexual from heterosexual men and women. The Terman-Miles test for masculinity and femininity was better but could not differentiate active homosexual males from normal males. In this instance *active* indicated those homosexuals who took a dominant role. Neither have draw-a-person tests differentiated homosexuals from normals.

The Rorschach test does not differentiate men from women, nor are there any responses that differentiate the homosexual male from the normal male. The Thematic Apperception Test (TAT) in the hands of a skilled clinician may be "satisfying," but when uniform scoring methods are used, they do not provide significant information regarding sexuality. The TAT does, however, provide increased understanding of the dynamics of homosexuality.

The Dynamic Personality Inventory (DPI) revealed that homosexuals are more emotionally dependent and narcissistic and more frequently have a greater difference in their masculinity and femininity scores. There was no mention of the incidence of psychopathology in homosexuals in Grygier's article.

Two recent studies by Siegelman have inquired into the psychological adjustment of homosexual and heterosexual men.[33] Siegelman used several tests, including the adjustment questionnaires of Schier and Cattell; the Neuroticism Questionaire (NSQ); the Alienation and Trust measures of Streuning and Richardson; the Dignan scales of Goal-Directedness, Self-Acceptance, and Sense of Self; a Dependency test by Comry; a Nurturance test by Harvey and others; and a Neuroticism measure by McQuire. Femininity was measured by the Gough Femininity Scale. Finally, he used the Crown-Marlowe Social Desirability Scale (SDS) and Socioeconomic Index. To indicate the depth of his study, I have listed the wide variety of tests that he used.

Siegelman's results demonstrated that, when compared with heterosexual males, the homosexuals were more submissive, tender-minded, anxious, and nurturant and had a greater sense of self. There was no difference in depression, alienation, trust, goal-directedness, self-acceptance, and neuroticism. He divided his homosexual and heterosexual male groups into those with low and high femininity scores. When comparisons were made, statistically significant differences were found only in the scores for nurturance in the low-femininity group. In the high-femininity groups, tender-mindedness, self-acceptance, and nurturance were significantly different. He concluded that, in general, effeminate homosexuals were more neurotic than the heterosexual population. This was interpreted as being due to cultural pressures.

An earlier indepth series of psychological evaluations of homosexuals by Hooker using the MMPI, the TAT, the Rorschach test, and other psychological measures, did not conclude "that homosexuality was necessarily and invariably a concomitant or symptom of psychopathology. In many individuals no evidence of psychopathology was found." After reviewing other relevant literature, she concluded that the only significant difference between homosexuals and heterosexuals is in psychosexual object choice. Gender identity does not seem to be disturbed.[34]

To conclude this discussion, it is important to recognize that no psychological profile will differentiate the homosexual from the heterosexual. In general, the homosexual is not found to be unusually neurotic nor is there evidence of severe personality disturbance. Currently available tests do not indicate significant feminine orientation of male homosexuals. Gender identity and psychosexual object choice are independent of each other.

## Treatment

It is interesting that although some persons in psychiatry have taken the attitude that homosexuality is not a disease, they still write about its treatment. In one of the standard textbooks of psychiatry, Marmor writes that although homosexuals present themselves for treatment usually because of difficulty in attracting partners, break-up of relationships, problems in self-realization, various neuroses, and depression, most of them simply want symptom relief. Others are, however, unhappy with their sexual orientation and desire to function as heterosexuals.[35] Such a statement seems to imply that the individual sees himself as a sick person. The administration of treatment implies that therapists also see the individual as sick, for a procedure is being used to cure or ameliorate a disease or pathological condition. One is then hard put to understand the confusion that exists. Nevertheless, Marmor does state that homosexuality is difficult to treat because of the pleasure and gratification it brings. Successful treatment brings satisfactory changes in sexual-object choice in 20 to 50 percent of the patients treated. Prognosis is good in (1) young persons, (2) those with previous heterosexual experiences, (3) those with recency of onset of homosexual activity, and (4) those with aggressive personality patterns. Prognosis is especially poor in homosexuals who are passive and effeminate.

A variety of treatment techniques have been used. Individual psychotherapy has received the greatest attention because of the work of Bieber, Socarides, Ellis, and Marmor.[36] It may be carried out in conjunction with group therapy.[37] For the most part, therapists attempt to devalue homosexual impulses and actions while encouraging the patient to make heterosexual approaches. Socarides summarized the analytic treatment process as follows: First, it is necessary to interpret to the patient his fear of castration, then his fear of oral dependency, then his disgust with the opposite sex, and finally, his fear of his own destructiveness and sadism. Socarides goes on to say that the interpretation that achieves the greatest relaxation of the homosexual's resistance is that the homosexual act is an attempt to acquire masculinity through identification with the partner and his penis in the homosexual act. After this, the patient may be able to function heterosexually. Socarides emphasizes the need for motivation, if a successful outcome is to be achieved in therapy.[38] Socarides also summarizes in depth the work of Bieber and Glover.[39] Bergler also emphasized the need for motivation but pointed out that extreme dependence on the mother and the use of homosexuality as a weapon against the family make therapy almost impossible.[40]

The leading proponent of group therapy for homosexuality has been Hadden.[41] Others have reported successful treatment in groups alone or combined with individual therapy.[42] All authors emphasize the point that homogeneous group composition is a necessity if therapy is to be successful. There appears to be little difference in results whether group therapy is used alone or is combined with individual therapy.

The use of aversion therapy has been most adequately reviewed and investigated by Feldman and MacCullough.[43] Srnge and Freund have also used this technique.[44] Basically, the goal of aversion therapy is to establish an aversion to the homosexual object choice by showing pictures of nude males when the patient is nauseated as a result of the administration of emetine. Others have used electric shocks that were applied if the patient did not turn off the projected pictures of nude men in eight seconds. Immediately after the shock the picture of an attractive nude female was shown so that it could be associated with the relief of anxiety.

As with psychotherapeutic intervention, aversion therapy requires a high level of motivation. A patient must be willing to submit himself to a painful procedure. He must also be able to establish a strong relationship with the therapist. Aversion therapy requires that the patient as a person be involved in the treatment program. He must be encouraged to initiate or increase heterosexual behavior.

Masters and Johnson have used behavioral modification therapy with good success.[45]

Recently I have worked with seven male homosexuals and three lesbians.[46] The outcome of the therapy of these ten patients has been a successful reorientation of their sexual practices to heterosexuality in seven cases. Four of the male homosexuals and the three lesbians were reoriented. In evaluating these patients, I found that the classification or the degree of homosexuality was not a factor in the effectiveness of the therapy. The subjects were classifiable as exclusively homosexual (Kinsey Type 6), predominantly homosexual and only occasionally heterosexual (Type 5), and predominantly homosexual but more than occasionally heterosexual (Type 4). Those who had heterosexual relationships usually fantasied homosexual acts during intercourse.

All were Christians, and those who were successfully treated were (1) repentant (John 5:3–6), (2) wanted to be transformed (Rom. 12:2), (3) had faith that God could and would transform them (Phil. 3:21), (4) were willing to state their case before God in prayer (James 5:13), and (5) wanted God's will for their lives (Luke 22:42). With this understanding, I was able to treat the patient, using individual and group Christian psychotherapeutic techniques. These began with the standard methods of careful history taking and the determination of family dynamics and roles. I then attempted to ascertain the patient's relationships with other individuals and the influence of these significant persons on his thinking and behavior. In most instances the parents were available for interview and were involved in family therapy. This was important because the attitudes of the parents were a vital factor in the change that took place in the patient. When parents were able to assume their responsibility and be humbly willing to ask their son or daughter for forgiveness, change was more readily obtained and therapy progressed rapidly. In one family, in which the Christian father was a rigid, domineering manipulator, no progress was made.

Prayer was a regular part of both individual and group therapy sessions. Prayer content was determined at the end of each session by reviewing the material discussed and determining where action was necessary. Confession, repentance, forgiveness, and intercession were included in the patients' prayers.

One can find in Christian literature numerous instances of reorientation of sexual-object choice as a result of conversion. I have known several such cases, one being a dear friend who was healed when he was converted after ten years of perverse homosexuality. He has now been exclusively heterosexual for thirty-two years. That there are thousands of others is a certainty, but like my friend's conversion and reorientation, they are rarely made public. Therefore, Christian faith is therapeutic in the sense that it can instantaneously reorient the person or serve as a motivating force to bring about change. It is a viable therapeutic alternative.

## THE MASTERS AND JOHNSON REPORT

In the foregoing I have made an effort to review those biological and psychological aspects of homosexuality that I believe bear on the causes of this abberation. In it I have referred, where appropriate, to the recently published work of Masters and Johnson.[47] Much of their report does not directly relate to the material presented here. I do, however, believe that their work adds further support to the idea that homosexuality is a learned behavior and helps to disprove claims that homosexuals are "different" in aspects of their existence other than sexual-object choice. I have, therefore, chosen to summarize the relevant material in their report.

They have reported the results of a series of observations on the physiology, functional efficiency, fantasy patterns, and homosexual-response patterns of a group of carefully selected homosexual male and female subjects. These data were accumulated when they observed the subjects' response to masturbation, partner manipulation, and fellatio (oral sexual stimulation of the male) or cunnilingus (oral sexual stimulation of the female). Their subject groups included committed (not necessarily married) couples as well as assigned pairs. The results revealed that there were no differences in functional efficiency between homosexual and heterosexual men and women in response to similar sexual stimuli. There were no significant differences in sexual physiological responses. Fantasy patterns were not unique, and both homosexuals and heterosexuals commonly had "cross preference" fantasies. There was a difference between the attitudes of assigned couples and those of committed couples toward the enjoyment of the partner. Assigned homosexual and heterosexual couples most often moved toward climax as quickly and efficiently as possible. Subjective involvement in the needs of the partner was minimal. Results of the treatment of homosexuals using their techniques were uniformly good and were equal to those reported by other authors.

Ambisexuals (bisexuals) were for the most part self-centered and lonely. They seemed incapable of establishing meaningful relationships. Commitments by young homosexuals (21 to 30 years) of over one year's duration occurred in only one-third of the subjects.

## Conclusions

From the foregoing discussion it becomes clear that homosexuality is a problem of psychosexual-object choice. The experience of many therapists and investigators strongly implicates disturbed parental relationships with the child and significant others in the nurturing environment as well as between the significant others themselves. I use the term *significant others* because I have found that grandparents, uncles, aunts, cousins, and siblings can be involved. There is, then, good evidence that psychological factors play a significant role in determining their aberrant psychosexual-object choice and sexual orientation. There is no substantial evidence at the present to show that genetic or hormonal factors play a direct or indirect role in the development of homosexuality.

Homosexuals do not display significant psychopathological disturbances. They are intellectually normal. They do, however, have increased psychosomatic complaints that suggest the presence of conflict.

Treatment using dynamic individual psychotherapy, group therapy, aversion therapy, or psychotherapy with an integration of Christian principles will produce object-choice reorientation and successful heterosexual relationships in a high percentage of persons. Successful therapy is predicated on high levels of motivation, previous successful heterosexual performance, and aggressive masculine behavior. Conversion may instantaneously heal some persons.

One can conclude that although homosexuality has its origin in disturbed family dynamics during early childhood, it can nevertheless be treated successfully. Homosexuals can change their orientation. God has condemned homosexual behavior and has made the power to change available to those who desire it. Therefore, "homosexual and Christian" is a contradiction. Homosexuals have no excuse, but if they desire change, they do have hope.

# 5

# Civil Rights and Homosexuality

The author is a writer and a member of the Texas State Bar Association. He is a graduate of Harvard College, B.A. (magna cum laude), and Harvard Law School, J.D. Dr. Proctor has written more than a dozen books, including On the Trail of God, The Born-Again Christian Catalog, and Survival on the Campus, and is the editor of the Church Business Report newsletter. He is a lay leader and trustee in the Park Avenue United Methodist Church, New York City.

## By William Proctor

# Homosexuality

in the Old Testament
in the New Testament
in church history
in the physical and emotional
**in the courtroom**
in the church

**5** The homosexual controversy in our society may begin with moral and theological debate, but the final scene of battle often focuses on the nation's courtrooms and legislatures. As a body of law develops defining homosexual rights, Christians are often thrown into a quandary as to what action they should personally take in the legal arena. Should they join the active forces against gay rights? Should they only lend passive support to those who oppose giving homosexuals legal recognition? Or should they line up on the side of the prohomo-sexual-rights movement?

The answer to these questions depends on the individual Christian's attitudes toward homosexuals as a legal minority with interests worthy of being protected by the state. Should homosexuals, in other words, be accorded the same civil-rights status that our society is beginning to grant to blacks, Hispanics, and other national and racial groups?

The term "civil rights" refers to that body of judicial decisions and also statutory and common law which establishes certain privileges and powers *for every citizen* in a given community, state, or nation. Civil rights are often distinguished from "natural" or "human" rights, which apply to *all* human beings, regardless of citizenship. For example, some political philosophers would say that the rights to life and liberty are natural rights that all men should have, while the right to a trial by jury may be a civil right legitimately limited to a particular society. The interpretation of exactly what constitutes a civil right is constantly in a state of flux in the United States, however, as individuals and groups challenge laws and customs in the courts in an attempt to broaden their own powers and privileges.

Many gay-rights activists are working hard to achieve full recognition as a legal minority entitled to complete civil rights protection; and they have succeeded in changing the law of the land to some extent through federal and state court cases and various ordinances and laws. If they can successfully establish themselves as a minority entitled to constitutional protection, then their drive for improved legal status, including equal employment opportunities and homosexual marital privileges, will become a relatively easy matter.

There are several key areas that have been the target of advocates of gay rights. These include freedom of speech and association, personal sexual relationships, employment opportunities, and housing and public accommodations. A brief examination of some of these areas should give each Christian a realistic perspective on the success achieved by prohomosexual forces and also a basis for making personal decisions about precisely what rights homosexuals should have.

As far as the Bill of Rights is concerned, American courts have held that the First and Fourteenth Amendments give homosexuals the right to speak freely, distribute literature, and assemble and picket in support of their sexual predelictions.[1] But at least one federal court has upheld the refusal of a state university to hire a homosexual who was in the habit of speaking openly about his homosexual life style.[2]

In the realm of consensual personal sexual relationships, homosexuals have faced considerably more resistance. Many state law codes still classify sodomy, including both oral and anal intercourse, as a criminal offense, often with years of imprisonment as the maximum penalty. These laws, by the way, prohibit such acts between people of the opposite sex as well as of the same sex. Also, it is important to understand that it is not illegal simply to be a homosexual—the only thing that is proscribed is the commission of certain homosexual acts.

There is an increasing amount of criticism of these laws on the ground that any acts that are done in seclusion and do not violate the personal autonomy of any party involved should be protected by an inherent right to privacy of life style.[3] Also, some opponents of these sodomy laws argue that the police and district attorneys have enough work to do without having to arrest and prosecute people for acts that do not affect the health and safety of anyone but the consenting parties. The homosexual, the argument goes, should have the right to do as he or she pleases with another consenting adult as long as the acts are not done in public.

As legislators see these community attitudes shifting, changes have begun to occur in the various sodomy statutes. Arkansas, for example, used to have one of the severest sodomy provisions, with a maximum of twenty-one years' imprisonment for consenting adults who participated in the act.[4] This law was repealed in 1976, however, and now sodomy is treated like heterosexual intercourse. As with heterosexual rape, there is a severe penalty if sodomy is forcibly committed on another adult or on a person who is incapable of giving consent either because of mental incapacity or young age (less than eleven years old). But there is no penalty for sodomy carried on privately between consenting adults.[5]

But while the rights of the homosexual must be considered carefully, so must the rights of the majority of citizens. One argument against a general decriminalization of sodomy is that an increase in homosexual relationships would occur and this would result in an even greater incidence of venereal disease. But some reply that a recognition of homosexual marriage rights would lead to more stable homosexual relationships and actually help limit the spread of venereal disease.[6]

Another argument for retaining the sodomy laws is that the state has a serious interest in protecting the nuclear, heterosexual family, and taking the laws off the books might encourage the development of more homosexual relationships. The family in American society is of utmost importance because it educates young people and is the basic social unit. If criminal laws against sodomy are taken off the books, homosexuality may seem more acceptable to many young people and they may start electing homosexual over heterosexual relationships. The heterosexual family thus would be placed in an even weaker position than it is at the present time.

This rationale apparently made sense to a Virginia federal district court that recently upheld as constitutional a Virginia law prohibiting sodomy. In that case, a group of male homosexuals had attacked the Virginia statute as unconstitutional on the grounds that it violated their rights to due process of the law under the Fifth and Fourteenth Amendments, to freedom of expression under the First Amendment, to privacy under the First and Ninth Amendments, and to freedom from cruel and unusual punishment under the Eighth Amendment.[7] But the court disagreed with this reasoning and held that the sodomy statute is constitutional when applied to active and regular homosexual relations between consenting adult males who are acting in private. To support its decision, the court stressed our society's deep-rooted, Judeo-Christian antisodomy sentiments by citing Leviticus 18:22 and 20:13, which condemn homosexual relationships.

This court indicated further that such laws are suspect only when they encroach on acts within the family or marriage. The implication is that oral sex between a husband and wife may be all right because, no matter what an individual's personal moral views, such an act probably won't have any significant impact on the sanctity of family life. Oral sex between two men, on the other hand, tends to pull the participants away from sex within marriage.

Adultery, by the way, would be subject to attack on the same grounds as homosexual acts because extramarital sex is a threat to the strength of the family. As a result, it would be logical for the proponents of laws against sodomy also to favor criminal laws against adultery.

Some may object that all this smacks of "legislating morality." But actually, all laws presuppose a certain basic set of moral standards that legislatures and the electorate want to impose on society at large. Laws are enacted against murder, theft, and rape because decent citizens believe those acts are wrong and, if unchecked, will threaten the safety and well-being of the innocent. Others would argue that it is wrong to keep so-called victimless crimes like homosexual acts, prostitution, and adultery on the books because they don't hurt anybody and tend to pull our police forces away from more important, and perhaps violent, cases. But in fact, most of the crimes designated as victimless aren't victimless at all. Someone or some institution is almost always hurt. Prostitution, for example, frequently acts as a magnet for more serious or violent crimes, such as mugging and robbing prospective customers.

In deciding whether or not an act should be proscribed by law, a couple of key considerations must be kept in mind. For one thing, the need for laws with stiff penalties against victimless crimes is in direct proportion to the threat to the well-being of third parties. On the other hand, if the threat to the general public is marginal and an unrealistic burden would be placed on law enforcement officials, it may be best to leave some morally questionable areas of life unregulated.

There are differing opinions concerning whether private homosexual acts are a sufficient threat to the public interest to justify prohibitive laws. But in a democratic society, there is no such thing as justifiable passivity or neutrality. The apostle Paul says in Romans 13:1, "Everyone must submit himself to the governing authorities." Peter, echoing this sentiment, writes in 1 Peter 2:13–14, "Submit yourselves for the Lord's sake to every authority instituted among men: whether to the king, as the supreme authority, or to governors, who are sent by him to punish those who do wrong and to commend those who do right."

In a democratic society, Paul's and Peter's exhortations suggest that the Christian should participate in the governmental process by voting and influencing legislation and executive actions through lobbying efforts. This means that each individual believer must decide, after much thought and prayer, just how serious a threat he believes the homosexual-rights movement poses to the family or to other social institutions and relationships. If he concludes that the threat is serious enough to warrant legal action, then it becomes his duty to act decisively and forcefully to try to get appropriate laws on the books or to have existing laws enforced through the courts.

Despite the continued existence of laws that make homosexual acts a crime, gay liberation forces have had some success in other areas. In governmental employment, for example—and especially in public-school teaching—courts have held that a homosexual may not be denied a job solely because of his status as a homosexual. To deny him employment, it is usually necessary to establish a connection between his sex acts and his ability to perform his job.[8] Any decision made by state or federal authorities is reviewable by the courts to insure that the individual rights of procedural due process under the Fourteenth Amendment are not violated.

But there is still resistance in public education circles to giving outspoken homosexuals a platform from which to promote their views. The University of Minnesota, for example, refused to hire an otherwise qualified librarian who professed his homosexuality openly. In upholding the university, the appellate court said the librarian was seeking

> the right to pursue an activist role in implementing his unconventional ideas concerning the societal status to be accorded homosexuals and, thereby, to foist tacit approval of this socially repugnant concept upon his employer, who is, in this instance, an institution of higher learning. We know of no constitutional fiat or binding principle of decisional law which requires an employer to accede to such extravagant demands.[9]

The same rules have been applied in nonteaching government jobs. One civil service employee, for example, might not be dismissed, a federal court decided, unless a definite relationship could be shown between his unorthodox sexual conduct and the efficiency of his service.[10]

But there are limits to gay rights in these areas. In one recent case, another federal court upheld the Civil Service Commission's decision to fire a homosexual who refused to answer questions about his sexual conduct.[11] And in those cases where the homosexual employee openly flaunts his sexual behavior, and thus becomes a disruptive or otherwise unsettling influence on other people, he may lose his job.

One Wisconsin court, for instance, upheld the discharge of an avowed homosexual who was employed by the state as the houseparent for about a dozen mildly retarded teen-age boys. The court was particularly opposed to the employee's predeliction for wearing eye shadow, mascara, and pancake face powder to work. Also, he had, on one occasion, squeezed another male houseparent's leg, smiled, winked, and confided he had a date for the evening. At another time, he called a houseparent a lesbian in front of the children. The court in this case didn't uphold the firing solely because of the employee's homosexual status. The real problem, the judge said, was that his advocacy of a homosexual life style and overt activities in front of young boys and co-workers interfered with the proper performance of his job.[12]

Although homosexual-rights proponents have made some gains in public education and government jobs, they have not, generally speaking, extended their rights in private employment. Among the reasons for this is the fact that often there are no requirements for private employers to justify their dismissal of employees. Also, private jobs usually provide no regular appeal procedure similar to that of civil service jobs.[13] Finally, Title VII of the Civil Rights Act of 1964 does not appear to prohibit employment discrimination against homosexuals or others on the ground of "affectional or sexual preference."[14]

In addition to job discrimination, homosexuals also may face problems in acquiring private housing, passing immigration and naturalization requirements, maintaining a career in the U.S. military, and so forth. This is especially true if they are open about their sexual preferences. In general, then, homosexuals do not enjoy the rights of minorities such as blacks and other ethnic groups, and they probably never will without laws and ordinances from the local to the federal level to protect them.

Recognizing the importance of such legislation, gay-rights supporters are constantly pushing for local ordinances that outlaw discrimination in employment, housing, and other areas on the basis of "affectional or sexual preference" or "sexual orientation." They have had some success in getting local laws passed and federal legislation proposed to prohibit discrimination against homosexuals. But a recent public backlash has resulted in the repeal of gay-rights ordinances in such cities as Miami, St. Paul, Wichita, and Eugene, Oregon.

One legal problem with such terms as "sexual orientation" and "affectional or sexual preference" is that they are so vague and general that they may open the door to the major threat that nonhomosexuals have always feared—the possibility that pederasts and other child molesters may be allowed to move into positions of authority over children. Gay-rights advocates are quick to argue that most homosexuals are nonviolent and respect the rights of their sexual partners to choose a homosexual life style. But are adolescents and preadolescents, who may be somewhat confused about their own sexual identities, really capable of making mature choices in this area? And what about those homosexuals who are violently oriented? There are altogether too many kinds of "sexual orientations" that could be permitted by most of these proposed laws and ordinances. So, if any law is to be enacted, some qualifications and restrictions should be placed on just what is meant by "sexual orientation" or "affectional preference."

But aside from this problem of legislative construction, there is an even deeper issue. By enacting any law or ordinance favorable to homosexuality, citizens and public authorities put themselves in the position of condoning and perhaps even advocating homosexuality as a valid alternative life style. The question Christians must ask themselves is whether or not they want to align themselves with legislation that sets a moral tone for society that is diametrically opposed to their own convictions.

Much of the opposition to the enactment of gay-rights measures has come from religious leaders. In fact, the future success of the gay-rights movement may well depend, in large part, on how aggressively Christian groups oppose the recognition of practicing homosexuals as a legally legitimate minority. This explains why strong pressures are being exerted on churches to change their traditional antihomosexual position.

But perhaps the most significant role Christians will play in the gay-rights controversy is the way they influence community moral standards. The nation's courts, as well as legislative bodies, tend to respond to the prevailing moods toward community values. If the community seems strongly opposed to extending homosexual rights, government leaders can be expected to respond accordingly. On the other hand, if judges and legislators sense there is strong community support for gay rights, they are likely to interpret existing laws in that light. For example, the Massachusetts Supreme Court recently construed the state sodomy statute to incorporate evolving "community values" and ruled the law didn't apply to consensual private conduct (though the law still applies to forcible sodomy, as was the situation in this case).[15] This kind of reasoning tends to give the green light to gay sexual practices.

The courts have even cited the words of current theology to justify legal recognition of a homosexual life style. One New York federal district court, for example, held that a man was a person of "good moral character" and entitled to naturalization, even though he was a homosexual. The man, the court noted, had led a quiet, law-abiding life, and his homosexual relations were conducted in complete privacy with consenting adults and did not tend to corrupt the morals of minors. Noting that the Immigration and Naturalization Service relied in part on the Bible to oppose this homosexual's application, the court said that many parts of the Scriptures "require interpretation and that even eminent theologians have not construed them as condemning all homosexuality." To support this contention, the court went on to quote directly from a Roman Catholic theologian.[16]

The interpretation of prevailing community moral standards, then, will probably be the most important factor in determining whether or not homosexuals will be recognized as a minority worthy of full civil-rights protection. At the present time, legal authorities seem to regard homosexuality primarily as a chosen mode of conduct; in other words, it is not an immutable condition and, therefore, does not represent a condition worthy of civil-rights protection in the same sense that ethnic minorities do. But if homosexual marriage and other such practices are recognized by the churches, the rest of society will likely fall quickly in step, and the recognition of homosexuals as a legal minority may well become a reality. The federal Civil Rights Act might be amended to prohibit discrimination based on "sexual orientation" or "affectional or sexual preference." A homosexual right to privacy might also be recognized by the courts. Gay rights advocates could then begin to rely heavily on the equal protection clause of the Fourteenth Amendment of the U.S. Constitution to solidify their civil-rights position.

Christians who believe homosexuality is morally wrong and represents a threat to society's basic family values are thus left with three possible courses of action. First, through their presence and witness in the community, they can help maintain public social standards that uphold the family. Second, as citizens of a democratic society, they have a responsibility to cast their votes for measures they believe are consistent with their Christian values. And third, they may become directly involved in the fight against gay-rights legislation.

Whatever course the Christian takes, however, it is impossible to remain neutral on this subject. By failing to vote or speak out, the Christian becomes a tacit supporter of whatever movement or "community value" happens to be in vogue at the moment. And if popular mores are opposed to Christian morality, the believer may well become a silent supporter of values that are inconsistent with his deepest convictions.

# 6

# Ministry and Homosexuality

The author is Chaplain and Pastoral Counselor at Methodist Evangelical Hospital in Louisville, Kentucky. He holds degrees from the University of Illinois, B.S.; Asbury Theological Seminary, M.Div.; and Boston University School of Theology, Th.D. Dr. McKain was a consulting petroleum geologist for eleven years prior to receiving his theological education. He taught at Asbury Theological Seminary for 5½ years. He is a Fellow in the American Association of Pastoral Counselors and is a Clinical member in the American Association for Marriage and Family Therapy.

## By Wm. H. McKain, Jr.

# Homosexuality
in the Old Testament
in the New Testament
in church history
in the physical and emotional
in the courtroom
**in the church**

**6** Does the Christian have a ministry particularly to the homosexual? Many would insist that no spiritual mandate is given for a specific ministry to homosexual persons; the problems, principles, and call to Christian ministry are the same regardless of sexual orientation.

Contrary to the traditional view of homosexuality, some within the church now contend that homosexuality is a "glorious gift of God." They say that the church should welcome homosexuals without restraints on or questions about their sexual life style. Homosexuals should be ordained into the Christian ministry, some church leaders argue, and the church should sanction the so-called marriages of those homosexual persons whose relationship is claimed to be based on love, devotion, and personal responsibility. Further, some now believe that the church should sponsor sex education in which homosexuality is taught as a normal variant life style and that the church should encourage young persons to choose their life style, whether homosexual or heterosexual. Role models of both should be presented impartially.

Support for this position is gaining momentum. It is becoming more visible if not in fact winning the approval of more people. The number of homosexuals in the United States is estimated variously from three million to twenty million. They outnumber persons with heart problems and cancer. Literally tons of literature are now available on the subject, including a *Journal of Homosexuality*. Yet the church is very much torn over the issues. Homosexual religious groups have emerged and have formed their own organizations in both Protestant and Roman Catholic circles. Well-known theologians openly avow their homosexual orientation. Many Protestant denominations agonize over the issues and the current contention that homosexuality is a normal and God-given, or at least God-tolerated, life style. What the church concludes about the issue has many and complex ramifications.

The position of this study is that *homosexual activity is contrary to God's revealed will and does indeed present unique* needs to which the church must endeavor to minister. Such ministry must not only relate to the homosexual person but also deal with the broader issues created by homosexuality and society's attitude toward it. Whatever the exact number of persons in our society with a homosexual orientation, we can be sure they are many; therefore, the church cannot treat the issue casually.

However, expecting the church to minister to homosexual persons and to deal with the larger issues homosexuality presents may be somewhat unrealistic. For generations the church has had a largely repressive attitude toward sex in general. It has thereby abdicated responsibility to lead society in an important and critical area of life. Also it has fostered taboos that have generated much fear and guilt. Further, there is no doubt that the church's silence has also contributed to society's current obsession with sex; for suppression of a natural drive normally will lead to undue curiosity, exploitation, and compulsiveness.

The church is beginning to accept responsibility to deal with human sexuality. It is now doing this, but, as so often in its history, this comes only in response to a strong challenge from the secular world. Christian writers are now addressing the issues of human sexuality, but relatively few sermons are preached on the subject. Many, many believers remain guilt ridden and fearful about their sexuality. In one survey of a church group, a young married woman said, "I know sex is okay in marriage, but somehow I just can't seem to rid myself of my upbringing, which led me to believe it is wrong."

Can we really, then, expect the church to address homosexuality openly when it has only recently begun a ministry relating to problems of sexuality such as premarital sex and divorce? It is asking much of the church to demand that it suddenly reverse its attitude and respond without fear or prejudice to the issues raised in this book. Lacking a clear understanding of one's own sexuality places great stress on a person (or an institution) if one is to respond with wisdom and compassion to homosexuality in the church.

A second question that must be faced is, To what extent is the community of homosexual persons open to ministry from the church and what kind of ministry will it accept? Barbara B. Gittings maintains that

> the majority of homosexuals would not change even if they could. More important, they should not change even if they could. What the homosexual wants—and here he is neither willing to compromise nor morally required to compromise—is acceptance of homosexuality as a way of life fully on par with heterosexuality, acceptance of the homosexual as a person on par with the heterosexual, and acceptance of homosexuals as children of God on an equal basis with heterosexuals.[1]

She further maintains that ministry to the homosexual should be of the same types that are rendered as a matter of course to heterosexuals. Ministry should be supplied in a spirit of acceptance and "not in a spirit of missionary zeal to convert us to heterosexuality."[2] Many homosexuals believe that a change in their sexual orientation would violate their personhood and constitute a rejection of their spiritual calling. Upon reading the position and purpose of homosexual religious groups such as the Metropolitan Community Church and its Roman Catholic counterpart, Dignity, one observes that they believe they have a special ministry to the church. Their drawing apart into separate groups is only to enlighten the church. They are "working toward the day when it (MCC) can close its doors because the other Christian communities with love and understanding will have opened theirs to the gay people."[3]

These attitudes may not represent all homosexual persons. But it seems certain that there are many homosexuals who do not wish to convert to heterosexuality or be recipients of the ministry of the church if that involves a rejection of their homosexual practice. Charles Schulz, in one of his recent "Peanuts" cartoons, points to the issue in his usual inimitable way. Linus is endeavoring to help Lucy get over her crabby feeling by pampering her and bringing her a snack. Then in response to his question about whether or not there is anything he has forgotten, Lucy says, "Yes, there's one thing that you haven't thought of. . . . I don't wanna feel better." Likewise, much of the homosexual community may not want the ministry of heterosexuals if it means a change of life style.

## MINISTRY IS TO NEEDS

Ministry is shaped by a perception of the needs of the persons to whom ministry is proposed. This is the key in considering ministry to homosexual persons.

### What Is a Homosexual Person?

We will look at those needs, but first we must define what we mean by a "homosexual person." For our purposes it is not necessary to attempt a comprehensive definition that takes into account the many factors of causation, patterns of homosexual practiçe, and the personality of the homosexual. It is enough to say that a homosexual person is an individual who is motivated in his or her adult life by a definite preferential erotic attraction to members of the same sex and who usually, but not always, engages in overt sexual relations with persons of the same sex. Reference to adults in this definition excludes the occasional adolescent experimentation the pastor may encounter in his youth group. Definite preference to the same sex excludes persons in situations such as prisons where there is little or no opportunity for heterosexual expression. Also, this working definition indicates that a homosexual person may or may not engage in overt homosexual relations. What, then, are the needs of such persons?

C. H. Patterson and others maintain that there are five basic questions that counselors must face as they approach the task of helping others. These are related to the question of needs. They are:

1. What is the nature of human nature, the nature of man?
2. What is the nature of human development?
3. What is the nature of the "good life" and "the good"?

4. What is the nature of the determination of the "good life"? Who determines what is good?

5. What is the nature of the universe, and what is man's relationship to that universe?[4]

All these questions, of course, are pertinent to our considerations. But those related to the "good life," the authority for one's views on the good life, and one's views on man's relationship to the universe are particularly relevant.

There are many today who suggest that a homosexual orientation can be as compatible to the good life as a heterosexual orientation. Some even believe it to be superior and more mature. In fact, the claim is made that homosexual persons make positive contributions to society that are unique.[5]

The Kinsey studies raised public consciousness concerning the incidence of homosexuality. However, three other major developments in recent years have lent support for prohomosexual views. These developments have come from the church, the legal profession, and the sciences. In 1957 the Quakers in England appointed a special committee to study homosexuality. The results of that study were published in 1963 in a pamphlet entitled "Towards a Quaker View of Sex." Although the pamphlet was the opinion of the committee only and not an official statement of the Society of Friends, it is quoted as authority in most prohomosexual writings. Essentially the committee held that homosexuality is natural and morally neutral, can be used for either good or evil, and should be judged not by its outward appearance but by its inward worth.

In 1966 a bill passed into British law also was considered a breakthrough for homosexuals. This bill, which was basically an enactment of the Wolfenden Report, stipulated that homosexual behavior between consenting adults in private should no longer be a criminal offense. Although this legislative reform was not a declaration concerning the morality of homosexuality, it has served as a reference point for declaring that under some circumstances homosexual practice is legal and therefore socially acceptable.

187

In December 1973 the Board of Trustees of the American Psychiatric Association voted to eliminate homosexuality from its official *Diagnostic and Statistical Manual of Mental Disorders.* The supporters of this action interpreted it to mean that homosexuality henceforth would be considered a normal form of sexual activity rather than deviant. Therefore, the homosexual person who was to be considered disturbed would have to be considered so on some other basis than sexual orientation. Charles W. Socarides and other members of the American Psychiatric Association seriously questioned both the wisdom and the tactics involved in this move. Socarides has implied that the change came about because of pressure from the National Gay Task Force. Further, he held that even though the change passed by a majority vote of the members who voted on the issue, the action may not have represented the true views of the total membership.[6] Subsequent surveys of psychiatrists lends credence to these suspicions. In 1977, 2,500 psychiatrists were asked if they thought homosexuality was usually a pathological adaptation. Sixty-nine percent responded yes, 18 percent said no, and 13 percent were uncertain.[7] Nevertheless, the impact of the APA change is an important reference for those who believe homosexuality is a natural variant.

In addition to these major developments, there are "authorities" from science with their aura of infallibility who are maintaining that homosexuality is "normal." Among these is Evelyn Hooker of the University of California at Los Angeles. In 1954 Hooker received a grant from the National Institute for Mental Health to study homosexuality. For those initial studies she selected a group of sixty men, thirty homosexual and thirty heterosexual. She then administered personality tests to each man. Experienced clinicians were asked to look at the results and rate the men on a scale of personality adjustment. Hooker's assumption was that if homosexuality is a sickness, it would be evidenced by the personality tests. Her studies showed that there was no difference in the emotional adjustment of the groups. Continued study has not caused Hooker to change her position. Paul Chance reports in an interview with Hooker—which he incidentally entitled "*Facts* That Liberated the Gay Movement" (italics mine)—that she now declares, "One thing we know for sure is that homosexuality is not, in itself, evidence of mental disorder—in men or women."[8]

Another study that is receiving considerable publicity is that reported by Alan P. Bell and others of the Institute for Sex Research at Indiana University, the institute founded by Alfred C. Kinsey. In these studies Bell and his associates endeavored to interview several thousand homosexual and heterosexual persons from all walks of life. These interviews took place in 1970. The authors conclude that "homosexual adults who have come to terms with their homosexuality, who do not regret their sexual orientation and who can function effectively sexually and socially, are no more distressed psychologically than are heterosexual men and women." One review of the publication of the report of their research headlined it "Study Finds Many Gays Are Well Adjusted."[9]

These studies by Hooker, Bell, and others are significant because they are efforts to study homosexuality *in situ* and not just in the counselor's room. By contrast, most earlier studies were based on the reports of therapists who had contact only with those homosexual persons who were distressed enough to seek help. Hooker, Bell, and others are endeavoring to study homosexuality among those who feel no need of therapy. The results of these studies are being interpreted—particularly by those who are prohomosexual and by others who are not aware of the issues—to mean that homosexual activity is compatible with the good life. The authority for these assumptions is the god of empirical research and statistical analysis. These reports come from experts in their fields, reputed scholars and scientists. Their research is done diligently and analyzed carefully. Therefore, their conclusion that homosexual persons are as well adjusted as heterosexual persons lends credence to the opinion that homosexuality can be a normal variant expression of sexuality and compatible with the good life.

Two presuppositions lead to such conclusions: (1) personality tests can measure mental health and (2) mental health and emotional adjustment are synonymous with the good life. These are critical presuppositions. It is like the small boy who ran into the house and declared to his mother that he was eight feet tall. When asked how he knew that, he responded, "Because I have just measured myself with this little ruler I made." It is exactly at this point that we must be cautious—when man measures himself by his own measuring devices.

## What Is Normalcy?

Even when we use our own rulers, mental health is an elusive object, and there are varying opinions as to what it is. Paul Tournier made this point when speaking on mental health at McCormick Seminary in Chicago. He quotes Claude Weil, former secretary of the General Congress of the World Health Organization for Mental Health, who said that the question of the definition of mental health has been much discussed and debated but has never been resolved in a satisfactory manner. Weil says that as a general rule it is easier to define negative concepts than positive ones. Thus, adds Tournier, "the most important treatises on medicine start with the subject of pathology, and during the whole of his life a doctor is constantly endeavoring to bring man to normality, without ever knowing precisely what a normal man is. He endeavors to bring healing and health to man, without ever knowing precisely what healing and health are."[10]

Tournier observes that Freud's goals in psychoanalysis were to "give a man the capacity to enjoy and to work."[11] Tournier contends that we must add to these some criteria of human plenitude, fulfillment, and flowering.

Tournier said also that Henri Duchesne, one of the founders of the International League of Mental Health, has three criteria for mental health: adaptation to one's milieu, acceptance of sexuality, and aptitude and talent for happiness. The two latter, he observes, are similar to Freud's criteria. The criterion of adaptation to one's milieu is the one that Tournier believes is problematical. It is the most critical criterion in considering the reports of Bell, Hooker, and others that lead to conclusions that adaptation and adjustment are synonymous with the good life.

Tournier reminds us that man is more than body and psyche. He is also spirit. Spirit is not a separate entity from body and psyche; it is that which connects man with God. Since man is spirit, any consideration of the good life must take spiritual health into account as well as mental health and physical health. This is where the problems get difficult, for the spirit of man is constantly striving toward fulfillment in a fallen and disordered world. In that striving the spirit must express itself in the world through the body and the psyche. Tournier holds that there is a hierarchy in this relationship—the spirit over the psyche and the psyche over the body. "Life," then, he says, "is built of movement and perpetual struggle."[12] Ideal balance or adaptation, therefore, is almost the negation of life. This is because the spirit would, of necessity, be adjusting to a disordered milieu. "Perhaps you will in those circumstances, enjoy mental health, but you will not enjoy or know health as a person," he says.[13] At the same time, if the imbalance is too great between the struggle of the spirit and its milieu, that also can do harm to the person.

Many view adaptation and adjustment as a criterion for mental health. But they fail to recognize that adaptation to one's milieu is adaptation to a disordered state because of man's fallen nature and his existence in a disordered world. As the apostle Paul indicates in Romans 8, both the sons of God and creation are groaning to be delivered from bondage. "Neurosis," says Tournier, "is an effort to adapt oneself to a world that is unbalanced and out of order. . . . Illness appears frequently as an attempt to find a cure."[14] It does not provide satisfaction, however, for it is an attempt to provide adaptation to a disordered milieu. The treatment of symptoms of neurosis—and of homosexuality—without attention to spiritual health and God's plan for man is dangerous. It is dangerous

191

because the struggle and movement involved in the illness is an expression of the struggle of the spirit in a disordered world.

Tournier notes that the French surgeon Leriche has defined physical health as a "silence of the organs." If no sound is heard from the organs, then we assume they are in good health. Likewise, Tournier says, "we hear nothing of our complexes just so long as we are in psychological health." Perceptively he adds, "But what would spiritual silence be? One could say, indeed, that it could give us a species of animal health. That is to say, we would have a man deprived of precisely that which distinguishes him from animals: a certain problematic tension in regard to value problems."[15]

Disease, then, is an expression of the spirit bound to existence in this life in a milieu that is disordered. It groans to be delivered from a respite of infirmity and death. In the meantime God is leading through the spirit and its strivings toward a restoration of what was lost in the Fall. The believers have been predestined to be conformed to the image of His Son.

Mental health, then, says Tournier, is living responsibly before God in a disordered world which, of necessity, involves struggle and movement if there is life. "Probably true health lies in making use of one's illness in a fruitful and useful way, that is, to find a way of succeeding with one's neurosis, rather than of being ill with it."[16]

Applying these principles to the issues at hand, we see that psychological adjustment, or silence of the complexes, is not necessarily evidence of the good life. Indeed, it may be just the contrary if that adjustment of one's complexes is an adjustment to a disordered milieu that silences the spirit. Movement and struggle are stopped and the spirit is without viability. If one believes that homosexuality is a symptom of the disordered state of man and not God's will, then adaptation to that state cannot be compatible with the good life, no matter how silent one's complexes may be.

With further incisiveness, Tournier notes that health is equivalent to riches, and Jesus reminded us that it is difficult for a rich man to enter into the kingdom of heaven. If, then, those who are plagued with a homosexual orientation can accept their state as "dis-ease," which is a manifestation of a disordered world, that dis-ease can be the doorway through which they can enter the kingdom. However, the door cannot be opened by making adjustment to a disordered milieu. It will be opened by accepting homosexuality as a state contrary to God's will. That very acceptance will provide an opportunity for movement toward closer relationship with Him. It is those who have been the most plagued with pain or grief or limitation who have often given us the greatest contributions. If homosexuality is seen as good, however, the energy that might have been derived from seeing it as a conflict is lost. Also lost is the opportunity for an experience of God's creativity as one gains victory over his disease of a disordered sexual preference.

Not all authorities from the behavioral sciences believe that homosexual practice is compatible with the good life. Bieber, Bergler, Socarides, and others, apart from any theological consideration, contend that homosexuality is a deviant from the normal and represents a maladaptation of the personality. The reports from empirical studies are by no means unanimously prohomosexual.

## The Good Life and Sexuality

Tournier's insistence on responsibility toward God as a key factor in experiencing the good life is important in understanding the good life as it relates to sexuality. Responsibility implies expectations on the part of the one toward whom one is to be responsible. The task each of us must face, then, is asking what the Creator expects of us concerning our sexuality. Only in responsibly meeting those expectations can we experience the good life. Any variance is less than good, or worse, depending on the issue.

### God's Will Concerning Sex

The biblical view of homosexuality is explicated in other

chapters of this book. Two points need to be reiterated here, however. First, the Bible makes it clear, and on this most will agree, that sexuality is a gift of God. Its purposes are at least threefold: (1) procreation; (2) to be an expression of love and one-fleshness; (3) and to symbolize the most holy relationship known to man, the relationship between Christ and His church.

Little is said about the symbolic function of sex. Yet this function may be the most important of all. Most discussions argue for either procreation or an expression of one-fleshness as the chief purpose for sex. Actually, to be one flesh and to procreate are both callings of God; either may require priority in particular circumstances. But the issues become clouded in this technological age. It is now within man's power to produce life in a test tube and to participate in heterosexual acts without any possibility of conception. However, we are called to be stewards of the marvelous gift God has given us, and its usage may vary with God's particular calling to each of us.

Nevertheless, God has revealed His will concerning certain boundaries within which we shall express our sexuality. Those boundaries confine sexual expression to the context of a heterosexual marriage—not before marriage, not outside of marriage, but in marriage between two people of the opposite sex. There are Bible verses that explicitly condemn homosexual practice. As a matter of fact, everywhere homosexuality is discussed in the Bible, it is forbidden. It should be noticed also that the Scriptures everywhere affirm heterosexual love in marriage as the context in which God expects us to express our sexuality. True, Jesus did not speak to the issue of homosexuality. He did, however, affirm God's will for heterosexual marriage and the goal of one-fleshness. As Bennett J. Sims has written in a very fine article, sexuality "is not humanity's gift to itself; it is God's bestowal and it carries conditions."[17] The Giver of this gift has declared the bounds within which we shall use it. To exercise this gift in a homosexual context is clearly outside the bounds of God's revealed will.

The mystical symbolism of marriage as a representation of

the relationship between Christ and His church involves both the concept of one-fleshness and the fact that man is created in the image of God. Therefore, Sims states,

> in regard to the image of God it is crucial to any Christian understanding of sex that the divine image in humanity is incomplete without both man and woman. Which is to hold that the aim of Christian sexuality is not personal satisfaction but interpersonal completeness. "The two shall become one flesh" (see Gen. 2:24 and Mark 10:8). This is the ancient prescription. One plus one equals one: completeness. It remains a great mystery since human experience is imperfect, even in rapture. But from the mystery we can discern the meaning of the ideal of completeness, which is *the union of opposites,* or the coming together of differences (though this is fundamental to a biblical understanding of sexuality), but such differences as personality, temperament, social function, and aspiration, all gathered in physical symbol of genital differentiation.[18]

The natural conclusion to this position is that homosexuality is a distortion of the divine intent and therefore contrary to any conception of the good life and sexuality.

It needs to be seen further, however, that whether one's orientation is homosexual or heterosexual, there are continual tensions inherent in being steward over one's sexuality. For the single, the married, and the have-been-married, the guidelines are the same as far as context is concerned. Therefore, if one's lot in life does not afford opportunity for sexual expression within God's prescribed boundaries, then the door to sexual expression with another human being is closed regardless of the sex of a partner chosen. Even in the context of heterosexual marriage, the need for stewardship in the expression of sexuality is not waived. All of the principles of loving one's neighbors and relating to them in the way that best fulfills them personally apply. And one's mate is, after all, one's closest neighbor. There is no room in marriage for lust, manipulation of the other person, selfishness, power struggles, control, and so forth. Therefore, homosexuals are not beings apart in humanity. They have no sex problem essentially different from that of other people, from that of the unmarried, the widowed, or the married. For all, it is the same problem, namely, that of absolute obedience to God's will, in sex as in all other domains of life. A man who by a look "commits adultery in his heart," to use Christ's words, or a man who uses his wife otherwise than as God's wills, is as disobedient, as sinful, as a homosexual who gives free play to his abnormal impulses. It can be quite as difficult for a married heterosexual really to obey God's will for his sexual life and to be absolutely pure in marriage as it is for a bachelor or a homosexual to observe an absolute sexual discipline.[19]

Our sexuality is a God-given gift, like a fire in the home. In the fireplace the fire warms and fills the atmosphere with tranquillity by its flickering light and pleasant crackling. In the attic, however, it becomes a roaring rage that ravishes and eventually destroys the home it was intended to comfort. When we use our sexuality outside of the clear, God-given conditions stated in the Scriptures, our experience of the good life is thwarted, whether we recognize it at the moment or not. When women exchange natural relations for unnatural and men are consumed with passion for one another, they will receive "in themselves the due penalty for their perversion" (Rom. 1:27).

## Should Scripture Be Reinterpreted?

These theological positions are criticized by those who interpret the Scriptures in a way that approves homosexual behavior if it is judged to be responsible, committed, and loving. Those viewing homosexuality as unscriptural will be accused of having a legalistic view of the Scriptures rather than the more humane, sympathetic view. They will be accused of needing a traditional peg on which to hang moral judgments. They will be charged with making a literalistic interpretation that takes no account of the times in which the Word was written or of the intent of the authors. It will be said that they employ an act-centered methodology as opposed to a situation-centered methodology of interpretation. They will be rebuked for suppressing humanity's dynamic and self-creative freedom in favor of static essence.

These critical comments express points of view that need to be heard. They have a degree of merit. It is also true that one's position on the issue of homosexuality rests on certain assumptions conditioned by one's view of the Bible, one's sexual orientation, and many other factors. However, those holding a traditional view on homosexuality need to be aware that the emotional and the rational appeal of these criticisms do not make the criticisms valid.

Many today are influenced by the empirical studies on homosexuality and have been led thereby to reshape their biblical interpretations of the matter. This is not ipso facto an error. We need to be open to reshaping our views if new understanding brings new light. But we need to be careful to look at all the available information. For instance, it has been noted that studies indicate there is no correlation between psychological adjustment and sexual orientation. But in some of that research there are other statistics that also need to be considered.

## Statistics on Homosexuality

For instance, the Bell research discussed previously also revealed that of the 979 homosexual persons with whom they had two- to five-hour interviews, 25 percent believed that homosexuality was an emotional disorder and about one-third had seriously considered stopping all homosexual activity at some point in their lives. Further,

the average male (homosexual person) reported sex acts with hundreds of men, and two-thirds had developed venereal disease at least once. Forty percent of the men had had more than 500 sex partners, and a quarter of them, as adults, had performed sex with boys under 16.[20]

These statistics vary between whites and blacks, and the Bell study indicated that 50 percent of the white homosexual males had had over 500 different sexual partners.[21] In another place

Bell made the following comment about their research:

> A modal view of the white male homosexual, based on our findings, would be that of a person reporting 1,000 or more sexual partners throughout his lifetime, most of whom were strangers prior to their sexual meeting and with whom sexual activity occurred only once. Only a few of these partners were persons for whom there was much care or affection or were ever seen socially again. During the past year, twenty-eight percent reported having had more than fifty partners; however, thirty-one percent claimed to have had ten partners or less.[22]

Dr. Walter H. Smartt, head of the department of venereal diseases in Los Angeles County, has reported that 50 percent of the syphilis and 20 percent of the gonorrhea in Los Angeles County is accounted for by homosexual persons.[23]

An Associated Press release from London on 12 June 1972 quoted Dr. R. D. Catterall, head of the Middlesex Hospital's Department of Venereal Disease, as writing,

> In some large cities such as London, New York, Copenhagen, and Paris, more than half of the infectious syphilis seen in hospitals is occurring in homosexual men, many of whom are quite young. Homosexual men tend to be very promiscuous and change their sexual partners frequently. It is still believed that it is impossible to be infected by homosexual relationships. In fact, it is just the opposite of the truth, and today homosexual men form a group which has one of the highest incidences of sexually transmitted diseases in the world.[24]

A 1978 news item noted:

> The latest on the homosexual front: an English group, the Paedophile Information Exchange, consisting almost exclusively of male homosexuals, is calling for the legal and social acceptance of paedophilia (sex with children), the recognition of what it calls "the need in Britain for a group of men and women sexually attracted to young people," and the lowering of the age of consent.[25]

I once heard a seminary professor comment that "there are lies ... and statistics," indicating that statistics are sometimes employed selectively. It is admitted that the statistics related to homosexuality, promiscuity, venereal disease, seduction of children, and so forth, are subject to various interpretations. The point is, however, that the headliners who write that "gay is good" and the manufacturers of "Gay Bob" dolls (for all people who want to be liberated and come out of their closets) don't mention all of the statistics. It seems to require special skill in mental gymnastics to reconcile some statistics related to homosexual experience with the good life. Again, as Romans 1:27 indicates, there is a due penalty for the error of homosexual practice.

## The Character of Love

Those who hold that homosexual practice is compatible with the good life appeal to the character of love. The church is asked to reverse its condemnation of homosexual practice and endorse it because homosexuality can be an appropriate expression of Christian love. Also, the appeal to love is used in an effort to instill guilt in those who disagree. As Muehl has so aptly stated, when anyone refuses to endorse the demands of the homosexual militants today and "presumes to suggest that this proposal requires careful examination and the review of a number of substantive theological issues, he or she is very likely to be accused of loveless bigotry and charged with causing great pain to some very sensitive people."[26] The appeal is that truly loving a homosexual person requires accepting homosexual practice. The fallacy in that appeal is obvious.

Love constrains us to relate to others according to their needs. However, that prescription sometimes requires me to relate to my children, my wife, or my friends in ways that they do not prefer because love may not lead me to see their needs in the same way they do. Sometimes the need is to comfort my friend. Sometimes the need is for me to leave him in his solitude. Sometimes the need is for me to resurrect a conflict that stands in the way of our relationship and thus stay by his side when he would prefer me to leave. Loving behavior obviously cannot always be determined by the desires of the loved object. But, as Muehl also writes, " 'God is love'—so runs the argument. Anything that is an expression of love is good. Since same-gender sex is an expression of love, it should be blessed by the church."[27] He tags this as a "classic example of question-begging" and then states further, "One of the most popular errors in the realm of Christian ethics has been the effort to make love an omnipotent spiritual quality which has the power to sanctify anything that is done in its name."[28]

Love does not give us license to transcend the requirements of responsibility in our relationships but rather requires us to express ourselves in appropriate and certain ways. Indeed, Muehl summarizes,

> Love *establishes* the modes of interpersonal relating. It does not simply consecrate those that we find pleasant or profitable.
>
> Thus, love does not always justify sexual union. It frequently makes it clear that sexual union is grossly inappropriate to a relationship. It is wrong for fathers to act out their love for their daughters in coition, for mothers to take their sons to bed, for brothers and sisters to copulate. Only the sickest minds would hold otherwise. And once we have established that fact the argument that homosexual union is good simply because it is motivated by love falls of its own weight. It is every bit as likely that the love of man for man or woman for woman bids them refrain from sexual intercourse as that it urges them into it.
>
> For the purpose of making such statements about the argument that same-gender sex is an expression, however inappropriate, of love, I have assumed that some form of affection is, indeed, the driving force in gay relationships. This is by no means incontrovertibly established. A number of authorities in the field argue that the dynamic of homosexuality is not love for the same sex but hatred of the opposite sex. Men who take other men to bed, they suggest, may be less interested in expressing affection for their partners than in displaying contempt for women. And the same would be true, *mutatis mutandis*, for lesbians.[29]

It becomes obvious that there is a clear relationship between true love, responsibility, and the good life that the Creator has revealed to us. It also is obvious that any views on the good life will inevitably involve certain a priori faith assumptions.

### MINISTRY TO HOMOSEXUAL PERSONS

Doing what comes naturally is not necessarily the pathway to the good life, whether one is talking of sexuality or any other dimension of life. Rather it is responsibility that is the key factor. This applies to a consideration of ministry as well. If one views homosexuality according to the position expressed in this book, the natural tendency may be to condemn homosexual practice as well as persons who have a homosexual orientation and declare that we should come out from among them and be separate. That is, we should have nothing to do with the problem beyond rejecting homosexuality as contrary to that which leads to the good life.

### *Ministry As an Opportunity*

The unnatural, and responsible, thing to do is to see the current problems that the church faces because of homosexuality as an opportunity for God to do something significant through us. This is just the opposite of our tendency to be pessimistic because of the intensity of some of the problems involved in the issue. Because homosexual practice is seen by many in the church as a loathsome perversion in the midst of an already taboo area and because of the pessimistic prognosis for change heard from many quarters, it would be easy to despair and do nothing.

Writing out of the context of his struggle as an avowed but nonpracticing homosexual, Alex Davidson insists the homosexual person must put his or her sexuality in proper perspective. His insight is revealing:

> I believe it's common for homosexuals to be obsessed with their sexual predicament to the point where they can think of nothing else, and I see the tendency in myself. A balloon which needs to be pricked, my brother—a house of cards which will collapse before a gust of good sense and discernment, and humour, which our sol-

emn enemy can't abide. All these help to get things in perspective. There are more important matters in life than indulging in a good moan because one is made differently from one's neighbour. The neighbour may be envied for his blessedly uncomplicated heterosexual life, but he assuredly has some other burden he might justifiably moan about.[30]

The church likewise needs to develop a proper perspective on the problem. It should not throw up its hands in despair or hide its hands for fear of soiling them. The Christian gospel declares that God always does His greatest work in the most difficult situations. Davidson says in this regard, "When He [Christ] intends to make something wonderful He starts with a difficulty, and when He intends to make something very wonderful He starts with an impossibility."[31] The church should be optimistic and rejoice at the opportunity to minister to homosexual persons as a part of its ministry to the world. Out of the midst of a very difficult problem, God can do something significant. He can take our adversity and change it to advantage; He can work creatively in our conflicts.

If the church is to be responsible in facing the problems of ministry to homosexual persons, its first task is to learn more about the problem of homosexuality. It is incumbent on anyone and any group proposing to minister in this area to learn about homosexuality. As a matter of fact, it is unfortunate that, in this scientific age when God's gift of knowledge is so liberally given, the church has not utilized more fully His gifts of technology and science for His purposes. But it is not too late.

## The Etiology of Homosexuality

Most writers who survey the data and opinions available on homosexuality conclude with one voice that the etiology, or causes, of homosexuality is a complex matter about which we really know very little of any conclusive nature. It is not within our scope here to consider in detail the causes of homosexuality. A brief consideration of causes is in order, however, so that we may develop perspective.

Causes that have been posited can be arranged into three general groupings: (1) those related to inborn, or constitutional, factors; (2) parent-child and other family dynamics; and (3) external environmental influences. One of the main issues in a consideration of causes in any of these areas is the question, To what extent is the homosexual person responsible for his or her orientation?

Many homosexual persons contend that their sexual orientation is inborn and thus natural. Others studying etiology have conjectured that the orientation results from hormonal imbalances. In either instance, the appeal is to a natural genetic or physiological cause. Although these theories were popular among investigators earlier in the century, most experts now see little evidence that homosexuality is caused by either genetic factors or hormonal imbalances. Hooker states, for example,

> People are not born homosexual, but there may be a genetic predisposition. Or it may take an indirect route; physique is influenced by heredity, and boys who have frail physiques may be more likely to become gay.
> There is no evidence that homosexuals have faulty hormone levels, or that their sexual orientation can be changed with hormone injections. Hormone shots may increase the level of sexual desire, but they won't change where the desire is directed.[32]

Even if there were evidence to substantiate the position that some homosexuality is caused by genetic or hormonal factors, that would not necessarily dictate that homosexuality is a natural state. It could just as easily be interpreted theologically as an evidence of the Fall if it is believed that the fall of mankind is pervasive, and it seems obvious that it is, in the light of other congenital disorders that are unquestionably pathological.

One thing on which many writers are in agreement is the theory that the sexual identity of the child is formed at a very early age, perhaps as early as two years. The factors involved are considered integral to the process. In the case of a developing homosexual person, the most critical of these factors is generally assumed to be an abnormal relationship with one or both of the parents—a relationship that results in a distorted or arrested psychosexual development. Various interpretations of the interactions of the dynamics involved come from the views of Freud, Bieber, Bergler, and others.

Busby lists nine different patterns of relationship between parents that may contribute to a faulty psychosexual development: (1) absence of intimacy of the mother with the father; (2) the absent father, either by death or by divorce, coupled with a mother who is too "present"; (3) the punitive father coupled with a masochistic mother; (4) a passive father with a domineering mother who also relates to the boy in an overly protective or overly permissive way; (5) an aloof father coupled with a mother who is too close and overly involved; (6) a vulgar father coupled with a prudish mother, giving the child an impression that masculine sexuality is reprehensible; (7) both parents absent from the child before he is twelve; (8) the idealized mother coupled with a block in the child's identifying with the father, resulting in overidentification with the mother; and (9) the idealized father (or older brother), resulting in a kind of hostile-dependency relationship with the father.[33] The complexity of these interactions is obvious. When homosexuality is also seen as a complex adjustment that results in both instinctual gratification and defensive compromise to meet the demands of the superego, we see more clearly the difficulty of the problem.

Bell wrote,

> With regard to etiology, a preliminary view of our own data leads me to suppose that just as there is such a diversity of adult homosexuality, so there are multiple routes into this orientation, routes which may well account for differences in the way particular persons experience and express their homosexuality as well as the nature of their psychological makeup and social adjustment.[34]

Some think too much has been made of the role of the parents in causing homosexuality. Yet, no one seems to discount the potential influence of the home and the probability that it is critical. Bieber gives some comfort in his conclusion that it is practically impossible for homosexuality to result in a home where the child has at least one sound relationship with either parent.

The home also has secondary influence because it is in the home that all of us gain the first inclinations that condition our reactions to our environment. Therefore, even though we talk about environmental factors outside of the home, it needs to be recognized that morals, coping patterns, and so forth, are behaviors mostly learned in the home. At least they are most capable of being influenced by the home.

The environmental factors that have been thought to cause homosexual orientation vary. Seduction by an older sibling or an older adult at a formative period may be a factor. If a boy appears effeminate, his classmates may treat him in a way that inclines him toward a homosexual orientation. Children who lack confidence in their capacity to relate to the opposite sex may gravitate toward same-sex partners as a less threatening way to find intimacy. It is thought that in some instances parents' grim warnings about heterosexual practice and accompanying silence about homosexual experiences may lead a child to seek the latter as acceptable behavior. It also is believed by some that the current moral climate that tolerates pornography, glorifies illicit sexual activity, and even seeks exotic sexual perversions may contribute to homosexual orientation and practice.

Assuming that all of these factors may be influential in some individuals, it becomes obvious that there also may be some persons who have a homosexual orientation as a result of their own conscious choices. It would appear, however, that the majority of those with a homosexual inclination have acquired it through less-conscious volitional processes.

Most homosexuals seem to have been passive recipients of their orientation and find themselves attracted to members of the same sex without the involvement of their own conscious processes. This point needs to be seen very clearly when considering a ministry to a homosexual person. It will engender compassion if the minister grasps the significance of the homosexual person as a passive recipient of an inclination involving pain, misery, frustration, and self-condemnation, as this problem so often does. This realization in no way releases a person with a homosexual orientation from responsibility of stewardship of sexuality. But it should cause sensitivity to the depth and complexity of the problem.

Such a realization also should convince us that the distinction between homosexual orientation and homosexual practice is entirely appropriate, even though the Bible does not explicitly make such a distinction. It appears to me that any concept of divine grace compels us to recognize that a homosexual orientation that is passively received but not practiced is not in itself condemned by the Scriptures. It is equally apparent that homosexual practice is condemned. The reader may have difficulty understanding the person who "finds" himself attracted to members of the same sex. The self-descriptive struggles of Alex Davidson[35] or some similar work by a Christian homosexual person may prove to be helpful reading.

### Developing an Acceptive Attitude

Ministry to homosexual persons compels us to examine attitudes toward homosexuals. John Patton reminds us that the term *homosexual* is an adjective, and if that adjective threatens us, we may not be able to respond in love to the person to whom it may apply. "Probably all of us," he writes, "have thus been overcome by adjectives and have failed to see the person who is looking to us for help."[36]

A negative reaction to the adjective *homosexual* indicates what some have termed "homophobia." Because of faulty understanding, aversion, projection, or other factors related to our own self-perception and sexual adjustment, we are prone to reject the person because of the label. The fact of the matter is, the word *homosexual* applies to only one segment of the person. It in no wise represents the whole person. All of us are much more than our sex drives and sexual preferences. Homophobia results in rejection of the homosexual person. This rejection may be conscious or unconscious and it does not really matter which. Rejection is sensed by the other person, and it frustrates the chances of ministering to that person.

Ministry requires on the part of the one presuming to minister the capacity to see the other person apart from his problems. It requires the capacity to see that person's inherent worth and potential as one who was made in the image of God and whose problems are no more, or no less, sinful that many which are common to all mankind. Such capacity requires a basic emotional health, a clear resolution of one's own sexual "hang-ups." This is a difficult task because reactions to sexual matters frequently spring from deep within. Noted at the beginning of this chapter was the difficulty of the church's response to homosexuality today, in the light of its deep suppression of sex in general. Our homophobia may be deeply seated also. It can relate to a natural aversion to that which God has forbidden. Also, some psychologists believe that the roots of homophobia are unconscious connections we make between homosexuality and barrenness and death. In other words, it is something that we sense is contrary to a fulfilling life for the individual and the race.

It is, at any rate, incumbent upon any who would presume to minister to homosexual persons that they work through their feelings and attitudes about homosexuality. This will be evidenced by a successful effort to separate the adjective *homosexual* from the person involved. God's love, which has been shed abroad in our hearts, demands that it be so.

Does this imply that acceptance of the person means adopting a morally approving stance toward homosexual behavior? Not at all. In the first place, it is impossible for one to set aside his moral convictions in a pastoral relationship. Don Browning has made it clear that all therapy, and we might add all ministry, takes place within an unavoidable moral context.[37] This context, as well as the moral convictions of the minister, will be an inevitable part of the dynamics of the situation. Whether or not ethics, morals, or theology are ever discussed in a context of ministry, the moral convictions of the minister will inexorably be communicated.

It seems incumbent, then, upon those who would endeavor to minister to homosexual persons to be completely open and honest about their own moral convictions regarding homosexuality and homosexual practice. In no way does this imply that those convictions may be forced on the other person. Even God adheres to the guideline that love does not insist on its own way. But one conveys a greater degree of acceptance toward others to whom one would minister when one is open about one's own feelings and convictions and honestly admits them. Such openness and honesty also would necessitate acknowledging one's lack of understanding about homosexuality as well as any feelings of homophobia one might have.

There are, then, two pillars in the foundation on which one must stand to presume to minister to homosexual persons: acceptance of them as persons apart from their problems (and sexuality may not be their problem at all) and openness about one's own convictions and feelings.

One also needs to guard against stereotyping homosexual persons. As the findings of the Institute for Sex Research at Indiana University indicate, homosexual persons are just as varied as heterosexual persons. Therefore, relating to every homosexual person is an idiosyncratic process.

Since all persons, including those with a homosexual orientation, are unique, ministry is always a unique process. Needs and motivations will vary. Consequently, pastoral care or ministry in other ways may not necessarily have anything to do directly with homosexuality.

## Ministry Is Shaped by Theology

One's theology of homosexuality will determine the boundaries and direction that ministry will take with a homosexual person. The importance of theology becomes apparent immediately when the position of this book is contrasted with, for instance, that of Norman Pittenger. His theology leads him to conclude that

> the church has enough theological assurance to move forward in helping the homosexual in his or her kind of union to live as faithfully and in intention as permanently as the heterosexual. That ought to be the purpose of our Christian counseling and our Christian dealing with the homosexual—not to call him a greater sinner than others, which he is not, but to assist him to become a great lover. I am convinced that a sound theological approach will do a good deal to bring about this day of acceptance, welcome, and support.[38]

What the church can offer by way of ministry to the homosexual person is limited if that person chooses to continue in homosexual practice. Such a life style is contradictory to Christian truth and, therefore, incompatible with the standards expected of those who are members of the body of Christ. Baptism, membership in a local congregation, marriage, ordination, and other ministries of the church that are privileges of those who are recognized as followers of Christ cannot be made available to an openly avowed, practicing homosexual person.

However, the practicing homosexual should be made to feel welcome at all church programs, including worship services and other group activities that are open to the general public and do not have membership in the local congregation as a prerequisite. The following statement in the *Discipline* of the United Methodist Church is typical:

> The United Methodist Church, a fellowship of believers, is a part of the Church Universal. Therefore all persons, without regard to race, color, national origin, or economic condition, shall be eligible to attend its worship services, to participate in its programs, and, when they take the appropriate vows, to be admitted into its membership in any local church in the connection.[39]

In the United Methodist Church, then, the general ministry of the church is available to the homosexual person, but membership is contingent on appropriate vows. Those vows include an affirmation of faith in God, confession of Jesus Christ as Lord and Savior, profession of the Christian faith as contained in the Scriptures, and the promise "according to the grace given them to live a Christian life and always remain faithful members of Christ's holy Church."[40] The *Discipline* further affirms that homosexual persons, no less than heterosexual persons, are persons of sacred worth. They need the ministry and guidance of the church and the spiritual and emotional care that the fellowship of the church can offer. However, the United Methodist Church's stance that homosexual practice is incompatible with the Christian life is made clear by this statement: "We do not condone the practice of homosexuality and consider this practice incompatible with Christian teaching."[41] This determines the direction of ministry the church may offer a homosexual person. To hold otherwise is to believe Jesus Christ justifies sin rather than the sinner.

If, on the other hand, the homosexual person is willing to repent of his or her sins and take the vows of membership as all other repentant sinners are expected to do, he or she should be admitted into the fellowship of the church. When that occurs, all the resources of the church are made available to him or her.

Repentance and conversion to Jesus Christ does not normally free one from homosexual urges. The homosexual orientation remains and may continue to plague the Christian homosexual person. That being the case, ministry to the homosexual person will take the form of helping that person either to convert to a heterosexual orientation and perhaps marriage or else to live a celibate life. If God's prescription for the life of a disciple prohibits homosexual practice, we need to have the faith to believe that one or the other of these options will be attainable to the homosexual person by means of God's grace. Through two millenniums thousands of single Christians have demonstrated that the celibate life is possible.

Conversion to a heterosexual life style may not be practically attainable by all homosexual persons. Nevertheless, this alternative should be offered as a possibility for anyone caught in the grips of homosexuality. Even John McNeill, one of the founders of the New York chapter of Dignity, the organization of Catholic homosexual persons, writes,

> Practically all authorities agree that the first goal of counseling should be to guide the person with a homosexual problem to a heterosexual adjustment whenever possible.
>
> The person who merely fears he may be a homosexual, or is attracted to the homosexual community, should explore every avenue toward the achievement of normal heterosexual capacities and relationships.[42]

The availability of God's grace for such a conversion is implicit in all the general scriptural promises of victory over sin and deliverance from its power. There is also an explicit promise in Paul's reference to deliverance from the sin of homosexuality in 1 Corinthians 6:11: "That is what some of you were. But you were washed, you were sanctified, you were justified in the name of the Lord Jesus Christ and by the Spirit of our God." God is no respecter of persons. If He gave grace to the Corinthians for this particular need, He will do so for others with the same need. Certainly hope is greater for such a change if the subject is a Christian and has the support of the church. In that instance the Holy Spirit empowers the person from within, and the body of Christ lends external support through contacts and relationships.

The informed pastor can probably help the average young person who is struggling for identity and who may suspect he is a homosexual but has not been involved in homosexual practice. However, helping the confirmed homosexual change to a heterosexual orientation will require the help of a qualified therapist, pastoral or otherwise.

Bieber and others have noted that age, extent and duration of homosexual practice, motivation, guilt, and other factors affect a favorable prognosis. Motivation is particularly important, since change involves struggle. This is true because of the depth of the problem and because homosexual practice satisfies the defense needs of the ego, releasing tension and giving fulfillment of normal sexual urges.

## The Goal of Therapeutic Approaches

We cannot here consider all the various therapeutic approaches to helping the homosexual person cope with his sexual urges or convert them to a heterosexual orientation. However, we might note briefly that there is at least one goal common to all therapeutic approaches, except perhaps behavioral approaches and pharmacological approaches. That goal is what Nouwen has referred to as self-availability.[43] Relating to oneself meaningfully always requires being available to self. This is, then, a common task in all therapy, a ruthless kind of self-honesty that enables one to become aware of one's true feelings. This is contrary to our normal way of relating to ourselves in our efforts to appear in an acceptable light, even at the cost of self-deception. Self-honesty is absolutely essential for the homosexual person in therapy, for it is only as one becomes aware of one's true feelings that moral choices can be made regarding those feelings. Contrariwise, the denial of essential feelings cannot but result in harm. Nouwen affirms,

> The gospel makes it overwhelmingly clear that Christ came to reveal man's real condition in all its greatness as well as misery and to challenge man to face it without fear. Christ invited man to take off the mask of his illusion of self-righteousness.
>
> He in no way judges feelings or emotions. He only asks us not to deny, distort, or prevent them, but to make them available for God's love.[44]

Acknowledging feelings also robs them of their compulsive power.

There are some pitfalls in working with a homosexual person who wishes to change his sexual preferences, however. The tendency is to focus on the sexual dynamics, forgetting that those dynamics are actually symptoms of arrested or distorted development. This maladjustment is, in all probability, related to deprivation of relationships and/or an inadequate sense of personal worth. Majoring, then, on the sex-object choice in counseling may be counter productive.[45] We agree with Harvey that "what the homosexual needs more than the achievement of satisfactory sexual relationships is an inner sense of personal dignity and worth and the feeling of fulfilling a purpose in life."[46]

Meaningful and supportive relationships and what Harvey calls a plan of life can help to meet these deficiencies. The body of Christ can offer a meaningful and supportive relationship as a group, and the trained pastor can offer a strong relationship in the counseling setting. The life plan is, however, an individual matter. Harvey's suggested life plan for the homosexual person endeavoring to live the Christian life includes daily meditation, corporate worship as often as possible, daily examination of conscience with stress on purification of motives, systematic reading of Holy Scripture, a carefully chosen confessor and guide, and involvement in works of charity.[47] Such a life plan affords value to anyone when adapted to his own faith perspective.

Harvey also suggests that homosexuals who desire to live a chaste life should form a "Homosexuals Anonymous" group.[48] He notes that homosexuals in therapy benefit from association with other homosexuals. He believes, further, a "Homosexuals Anonymous" organization could offer support not available in any other context. He grants the reality of the temptation and the moral danger of such involvement. But he notes, "Surely the dangers faced by most isolated, or noncommunicating, homosexuals are greater."[49] This is an interesting approach, obviously similar in potential structure to that of Alcoholics Anonymous and deserving further consideration by the church.

Another area of pastoral ministry is to the family of the homosexual person. Many factors are involved. It may be necessary to help the person with the homosexual orientation communicate his circumstances to his family. This is not an easy task, but it can be made more bearable if an understanding pastor is involved in the process.

This being done, it will nearly always be necessary to help parents deal with personal feelings about their son or daughter. Guilt is often one of the first reactions. Parents will assume that their child's condition is somehow related to moral failure in parental relationships. It is helpful if parents can be shown that there are many factors that may cause homosexuality. It is reasonably certain that no one factor can be pointed to as the sole cause. Parents also need to be helped to see that all children bear the scars of inadequate parenthood. Although the scars of homosexuality may appear more shameful to them, they are, nevertheless, no more grievous than those many children bear. However, the emotional reaction to homosexual practice is often stronger than reaction to other sins.

Parents should be helped to see also that they need to accept their son or daughter and endeavor to understand them. Only such channels of openness afford the homosexual person the very important family support that can help him or her work through the problems associated with their sexual orientation. Such family acceptance and understanding may require considerable pastoral care. Parents usually find it very difficult to respond positively to their homosexual child's needs. But acceptance for the homosexual person who has revealed his identity is extremely important. Rejection may only compound the problem. Howard Brown reports,

> Every year hundreds of disowned or runaway homosexual adolescents turn up at the office of the National Gay Task Force in New York City, looking for food, shelter, jobs; hundreds more roam the streets, keeping themselves alive by working as male prostitutes.[50]

It needs to be recognized that the foregoing comments are related to ministry to the male homosexual person. They may or may not be appropriate also to female homosexuals. Ministry to female homosexual persons may differ in some ways, since our knowledge of lesbianism is even more limited than our knowledge of male homosexuality.

Bergler and other believe that the guilt that a person may feel in regard to his homosexuality can be beneficial if its energies are mobilized in the therapeutic process. Traditionally, the church has been adept at raising guilt, sometimes falsely. Those endeavoring to minister to the homosexual should heed the warnings of McNeill, Szaz, and others who suggest that needless misery can be caused the homosexual person when a sense of guilt is over stimulated. In all probability, those coming to a minister with this problem are already suffering more guilt feelings than they can handle. It seems more appropriate, therefore, to refrain from adding to that burden but rather to offer the grace of forgiveness that God gives through faith in Jesus Christ and His atonement for sins.

Parallel with this precaution about guilt is that of being careful not to create unrealistic hope about the process of converting to heterosexuality. The facts are that not every homosexual person who becomes a Christian is delivered from his or her homosexual impulses. Many are, but we must face the reality that God does not always choose to deliver us from our infirmities—physical or psychological. Paul's experience with his thorn in the flesh, whatever it was, is a case in point. Conversion to a heterosexual orientation, then, may not be possible for everyone. It is certain, however, that God has promised that His grace is sufficient for us. His strength is made perfect in our weakness. His Spirit intercedes for us in our infirmities with groanings too deep to be uttered. Jesus Christ sits at the right hand of the Father interceding on our behalf. And in the final analysis, "If God is for us, who can be against us?" (Rom. 8:31). Therefore, even though we cannot give certainty about deliverance from the infirmity, we can give assurance of God's strength to cope with the infirmity.

In another vein, John R. Powell perceptively cautions about diagnosing a person as homosexual:

> Many young men not having accurate information about homosexuality as either a condition or a behavior erroneously diagnose themselves as homosexual. Such a misdiagnosis can set in motion a self-fulfilling prophecy that is consummated by tapping into the biologically rooted possibilities for bisexuality which

> otherwise would probably be passed over developmentally without difficulty.[51]

What is needed, therefore, is an accurate understanding of sexuality that allows for the fact that homosexual experimentation may be a common experience of children and adolescents that does not indicate a true homosexual orientation at all. Also, one needs to understand the distinctions that are made between true homosexuality and pseudohomosexuality as set forth in the work of Ovesey, for instance.[52]

### A Tension in Ministry

Let us conclude this section on ministry to the homosexual individual by considering a tension that obviously hinders any efforts to minister to such persons. This is the tension between a moral approach to ministering to the homosexual person on the one hand and the need for unconditional acceptance of that person on the other. These factors are usually polarized, but they need to be joined.

Sims notes that because homosexuality appears to be an adaptive step that is taken unconsciously by a threatened personality for its own protection, there are those who claim that it is immovably fixed as a part of one's being. Sims goes on to observe, however, that even Freud believed that a deviant act involved responsiblity on the part of the actor. If this were not so, therapy could not help anyone. Therapy involves helping the person see that he is not a victim of his circumstances. His choices in the past have had something to do with his present plight, and his past and present choices govern in large measure the direction of his life in the future. Sims then comments,

> Therapy that does not rest upon such an assumption must necessarily rest upon some other, which would be empty of moral content unless it held a person responsible for choices. Without moral content therapy is simply manipulative. It cannot respect the critical ingredient of moral freedom as expressing every human being's unique individuality. The important thing to notice here is that an amoral psychotherapy that seeks to absolve the sufferer

from moral responsiblity is not only anti-Christian, it is actually heretical to orthodox Freudian assumptions. Christian theology and Freudian psychoanalytic theory agree here. What this argument leads to is that unless the church is ready to challenge homosexual claims about the normalness of homosexuality, then the church in effect joins in reducing and degrading the humanity of the very people to whom the church needs to minister.[53]

Imperative, however, as this statement is, it must be kept in apposition with the fact that homosexuality is only symptomatic of deeper needs. These deeper needs relate to self-esteem and self-worth, which are only promoted in relationships and contexts where one is felt understood and accepted. That the church can play a critical role in this process, providing the moral issue is settled, is indicated by the following statement by McNeill:

> Logically, by his calling and his profession the clergyman should be the person to whom the homosexual could turn with complete confidence. And very often—some authors estimate at least forty percent of the time—the clergyman is the first person to whom he turns and reveals his problem. If, however, the homosexual should fail to receive a sympathetic reception, which unfortunately often seems to be the case, he could easily lose all hope. On the other hand, the very fact of being able to speak openly about his problem for the first time with a respected member of the community, who continues to manifest respect for him, can be an essential step toward establishing hope, where previously there was only despair.[54]

### MINISTRY AND THE BROADER ISSUES OF HOMOSEXUALITY

Beyond the ministry to individuals, the church also has opportunities for ministry related to the general issues presented by the phenomenon of homosexuality. These opportunities may be more far-reaching than the ministry to homosexual persons itself.

### The Homosexual and Civil Rights

One issue the church must concern itself with is the

217

homosexual's civil rights. That homosexual persons are being treated with prejudice and deprived of civil rights in some instances is beyond question. Jones cites the case of a soldier who, having homosexual impulses and fearing that he might become a practicing homosexual, sought the aid of a military psychiatrist. Instead of help, he received an undesirable discharge and his military service record became a hindrance for some time.[55]

Busby tells of a Baptist preacher from California who sought his help for overt homosexuality. This man said he was jailed in Evanston and confined with rapists and narcotic addicts. He reported that the police "glibly played cards with these other men, whereas they would hardly even speak with him and would push his food tray to him with their foot or even with a pole!"[56] Reports of such incidents could be multiplied thousands of times over. It is an undisputable fact that homosexual persons are deprived of some of their rights because of the prejudice of society toward the nature of their problem. The issues are frequently discussed in the literature of the day, and it is not within our purposes here to treat them in depth. We simply point out the necessity for the church to deal seriously with the problem.

The issues are complex. The common dilemma that faces the pastor is the conflict between the interests and needs of the homosexual person as an individual and the interests and needs of the community. Greenlee underscores this dilemma in his discussion of the Dade County conflict and the issue of whether or not a homosexual person has the right to teach in a public school:

> If a person whose standards of conduct differ from those of the community wishes to apply for a teaching position, so long as his actual conduct and words do not clash with those principles he may have the right to seek such a position, at least in a public school. However, if an applicant or a group of applicants declares openly to be significantly opposed to the standards considered acceptable by the school board and the parents of the community and demand acceptance *on that basis*, then it is no longer a matter

of the applicant's civil rights, but rather the civil rights of the organization and of its members to maintain their organization and its purposes.[57]

This tension between individual and community rights does not excuse the church from involvement. The church has traditionally been the defender of both and is obligated to wrestle with the many issues involved in the quest for civil rights of homosexual persons and of our institutions.

## The Church's Contribution to the Problem of Homosexuality

The church also must face its complicity in causing homosexuality. To the knowledge of this writer, no studies have been done in this area, but there are some factors that would suggest that as an agent of society the church has played a significant role in the prevalence of homosexuality. Most citizens of the United States at one time or another have contact with the church. For that reason alone, the church must accept some responsibility for the prevalence of homosexuality, either by default or by direct causation. Also, unquestionably there are many homosexual persons in the church. Those who counsel in Christian college and seminary communities find themselves dealing with a significant number of persons with homosexual problems. On the average Christian college campus, a chapel address that deals at all compassionately with the problem of homosexuality will nearly always bring a flood of persons to the counseling room for help. Counselors in such a setting sometimes wonder if the incidence of homosexuality is not greater on the Christian college campus than on its secular counterpart.

There are also some studies that indicate there are proportionately more homosexual persons among the clergy than in society in general. Jones quotes the statistics of one study that indicated that "of 4,040 sex variants studied, 1.6 percent were clergymen, while only 0.2 percent of the total male population are clergymen."[58] Simple mathematics suggests that the proportion of homosexual males in the ministry is eight times

219

greater than in the population as a whole.

Personality tests show that male seminary students score noticeably higher on measures of effeminacy than do their secular professional peers. Although these measurements do not necessarily indicate homosexuality, they do suggest that ministers present a more effeminate role model than does the average male.

Let us be quick to declare that these suspicions and limited statistics cannot produce clear conclusions. But they should lead us to ask what role the church has in causing or attracting homosexuality. It would be ironic indeed to discover that the church is unknowingly, but directly, contributing to a problem with which it is critically engaged at this time.

We can be sure that the church's repressive attitude toward sexuality over the centuries and the unfortunate taboos that have resulted contribute to the explosive power of sex in our society. Is it also possible that the role relationship between men and women in the church and its programs also may contribute to causing homosexuality? There seems to be no question but that the role relationship between men and women in the church varies from that of society as a whole. Through abdication by males, for whatever reason, the female is the more active leader in the church as a whole. Paul Tournier notices that there are more women in the church than men and speculates that this may have something to do with their differences of sensitivity toward morality. He suggests,

> The man is in general more conscious of his sins than the woman is of hers. He is very conscious of his sexual lust, of his lying to his wife or to his competitor, of his cheating on income tax, or of his excessive pride in his work. Perhaps this is one reason why he goes to church less willingly than his wife. He feels less at ease there. He feels a little pharisaical in thus publicly parading his piety, for he very well knows what is not right in his real life and what he does not feel capable of setting right. Perhaps this is also a reason why in church we see men who generally are less virile, little taken up in life's struggles: civil servants, teachers, men who can more easily lead a life apparently spotless.

Like such men, women generally are less conscious of their sins.[59]

No doubt such a statement will cause many women to rise up in arms. But Paul Tournier is no casual observer of humanity, and the fact is that in the church, by and large, more women assume roles of leadership than men. It also appears that the church draws certain types of men, as Tournier suggests.

## The Church's Role in Preventing Homosexuality

On the constructive side, we can be certain of some things that the church can do that may help prevent homosexuality, at least to the extent that such is caused by psychological factors.

Some have charged that the church has not changed its views on sexuality since the Middle Ages and that it has, in fact, ignored all subsequent data. This observation probably has some validity. There are those in the church, however, who are beginning to examine the knowledge coming from the behavioral sciences to see what light it may shed on a Christian understanding of sexuality. This kind of pursuit needs to continue. Those of the Christian community who have the knowledge and the gifts—the biblically trained psychologist, psychiatrist, pastoral counselor, and social worker—should take the initiative in sponsoring such studies. We have long been too defensive about knowledge from the secular fields. It is high time we began to demonstrate faith and confidence in the revelation we claim as authority and believe that it will stand without our defensive posturings. Such a faith and confidence in the Bible would allow us to be more open to truth coming through other channels.

A collateral responsibility facing the church is the need to take a more prominent role in sex education. Too often the church has been wont to criticize and resist sex education in our society. Only when it became obvious that sex education was going to come whether the church wanted it or not did the church begin to get involved. The church still lags far behind, however.

If we believe that there is a Christian perspective on the good life, then we believe there is a Christian perspective on sexuality. If we believe other views are deficient or limited, then it behooves us to proclaim the Christian view. There is a Christian view of sexuality, a view that holds that man is body, mind, and spirit. Any complete view of sexuality must consider that holistic perspective, because sex involves body, mind, and spirit. The biblical concept of one-fleshness and sexuality is the only perspective that leads to an exalted interpretation of man and his sexuality and whose prescriptions lead to fulfillment. Other views that reduce sex to the level of the sensual rob it of its true essence and the potential it has to serve God and man, not only in procreative ways, but also in recreative ways. The church should be leading those responsibly endeavoring to educate society about its sexuality. Such education should issue from the pulpit, the church classrooms, the home, and anywhere else the church has an audience.

There is no certainty among the experts as to whether persons are innately heterosexual, innately heterosexual and homosexual, innately homosexual, or born neutral in their sexual identity. Neither is it scientifically certain that they are predisposed in either direction. Most experts seem to suspect that sexual identity is a learned response or, even if it is innate or predisposed, can be skewed by the learning process. This leads Hiltner to comment,

> If you wish all persons to emerge in adolescence and adulthood with a dominantly heterosexual orientation, then you must study the complex factors that reinforce such an orientation and support them, while you also study the forces that lead to a dominantly homosexual orientation and attempt to decrease them.[60]

This suggests that the educational role of the church relates not only to sexuality in general but also to identifying and presenting models that lead to the formation of heterosexual identity. There is a need to induce positive learning toward heterosexuality and to limit negative learning in the direction of homosexuality. Calderone echoes this concern when she states, "Education for heterosexuality involves far more than education about the processes of reproduction or of physical mating; it most importantly is education about the roles of and relationships between men and women."[61] She maintains further, and I agree, that we can no longer take a passive stance in regard to this educational process:

> We can no longer depend on old patterns, or on "inborn" drive or on the simplistic moralistic negatives of our fathers, to achieve the goals we want. It is no longer even possible to trust the "instincts" of mothers and fathers to come through in the creation of the kind of stable family milieu that we used to look to for the production of stable human beings.[62]

She also recognizes the role the church can play in an informed educational process of sexualization.

The church has made, and is continuing to make, a concerted effort to present scriptural teaching about marriage and the family. This effort is vital and merits even more attention as we continue to try to understand Scripture in the light of current findings on sexuality. Marriage and family relationships receive considerable treatment in both Testaments and, as Powell has observed, "all combine to suggest a model of family life and child development which is the antithesis of many findings in the family patterns of homosexually oriented males."[63] Thus, the church with its resources of revelation is in a unique position to teach and model roles and relationships for wholesome sexuality.

Another model that the church could uphold is the witness of Christian homosexual persons who have either been able to convert to a heterosexual life style or have been victorious in living a chaste life. Such persons, no doubt, abound, and their witness could be of immeasurable encouragement as well as profitable instruction to others struggling with the problem. The church has long known the power of personal witness and so should elicit more such testimony from those who have found God's grace to be sufficient in this particular area of weakness. Naturally, there will be no such witness as long as the church reacts to homosexuality as if its practice were the most heinous of sins. Rather, as Paul indicates, it is on a par with greed, envy, deceitfulness, gossiping, slander, and other such common sins (Rom. 1:26–31).

Peter and Barbara Wyden note that there are many trends in modern society that could cause an increase in homosexuality:

> In brief, the once-hard line between what is clearly "male" and clearly "female" has been softening somewhat. There do seem to be more dominating, competitive women than there used to be. There also seem to be more men with weak masculine identity. There is a more healthy tolerance of sexuality in general, but there is also greater insistence on sexual "performance." There seems to be greater emphasis than ever on the value of achieving success in competitive situations (sexual, financial, athletic, etc.) and also, perhaps correspondingly, a greater fear of failure. Finally, there can be little doubt that the greater complexity of our society, the increasing rapidity of changes in the environment, the greater number of choices available to individuals in a wide variety of situations, all combine to produce more self-doubt. Never have so many adults wondered, "Who am I?" Never have children had a harder time deciding, "Who do I want to be?"[64]

The Christian gospel has a response to all of these issues and thus could be a powerful force in deterring an increase of homosexuality in our society.

## The Church's Need for Soul-Searching

To be heard, however, the church first must do some in-depth and ruthless soul-searching before it presumes to proclaim the answers in this area. The church must confess its own complicity in the problem and the destructive attitudes it has held. The church must proclaim with love its acceptance of all persons, regardless of the nature of their personal struggles, and guard against any appearance of self-righteousness. That will probably require a radical conversion of self-awareness on the part of the church with a sensitive ear to those condemnations of her by those of opposing positions. Their criticisms may not be totally accurate, but the opinions of one's opponents contain a modicum of truth. The capacity to hear those criticisms, therefore, can be an invaluable resource to the church in helping it respond to the issues involved in endeavoring to minister to the problem of homosexuality.

There is also the danger that fear of the struggle with the issues surrounding homosexuality will immobilize the church. Some fear homosexuality will divide the church. Others fear it won't. In any event, the Christian is required to believe that God can act creatively in the midst of conflict and that in coming to grips with the issues of homosexuality the church will experience new depths of spiritual maturity and certainty of the grace promised to it in the Christian gospel. As long as the locus of authority does not shift from the Scriptures and as long as Christians endeavor to follow its admonitions, they will experience the good life and have opportunity to lead others in their pursuits of it. Jesus Christ gave His life that humankind might have life more abundantly; He lives to lead His people.

I once had a colleague who had a way of putting issues into proper perspective. On one occasion we were discussing a conflict, seemingly caused by others, but affecting our circumstances. We discussed the persons and issues involved. Then he commented, "Well, I guess I'll just have to get closer to the Lord." That is precisely the challenge the church faces as it addresses itself to the issues related to homosexuality and develops a ministry to the persons involved.

# Notes

## Chapter 1

1. C. S. Lewis, *Miracles* (London: Fontana, 1960), pp. 38-42.
2. G. K. Chesterton, *The Father Brown Stories* (London: Cassell, 1948), p. 20.
3. Lucian, *On the Syrian Goddess*, tr. Herbert A. Strong, ed. John Garstang (London: Constable, 1913), p. 15.
4. This is not to say that a single person is less than fully human. It is to say that in the race as a whole males need females and females need males if the true potential of humanity is to be realized. All-male and all-female associations are bound to produce aberrations.
5. C. S. Lewis, *Screwtape Letters* (New York: Macmillan, 1959), p. 49.
6. W. Norman Pittenger, *A Time for Consent* (London: SCM, 1970).
7. J. D. Unwin, *Sex and Culture* (London: Oxford University Press, 1934) (Quoted by William Barclay, *The Ten Commandments for Today* [New York: Harper, 1974], p. 153).
8. Derrick Bailey, *Homosexuality in the Western Christian Tradition* (London: Longmans, Green, 1955).
9. See Marvin Pope, "Homosexuality," in *Supplement to the Interpreter's Dictionary of the Bible* (Nashville: Abingdon, 1976), pp. 415-17 for further evidence on this point.
10. Kenneth Grayston, *Theological Word-Book of the Bible*, ed. A. Richardson (New York: Macmillan, 1962), p. 12.
11. Bailey, *Homosexuality*.
12. Pope, "Homosexuality," p. 415.
13. For additional reading on the subject of homosexuality from the point of view maintained in this chapter, see William Barclay, *The Ten Commandments for Today* (New York: Harper, 1974), pp. 94-173; Carlos Castaneda, *The Teachings of Don Juan* (New York: Ballantine, 1968); Henri Frankfort, *Before Philosophy* (Baltimore: Penguin, 1949); Yehezkel Kaufmann, *The Religion of Israel*, Tr. and abridged by Moshe Greenberg (Chicago: University of

Chicago Press, 1960); G. Ernest Wright, *The Old Testament Against Its Environment* (London: SCM, 1960).

## Chapter 2

1. This passage is omitted from the best Greek manuscript tradition and is almost certainly not originally a part of John's Gospel; nevertheless, it is very probably a true story.

2. John V. Moore, "How My Mind Is Changing," in *Texas Methodist/United Methodist Reporter*, 28 March 1975.

3. Ibid.

4. Troy Perry, quoted by Harvey N. Chinn, *Texas Methodist/United Methodist Reporter*, 14 March 1975.

5. Moore, "How My Mind Is Changing."

6. William Robertson Nicoll, ed., *The Expositor's Greek Testament*, 5 vols. (Grand Rapids: Eerdmans, 1952), 2:831.

7. Ibid., p. 839.

8. William Barclay, *The Ten Commandments for Today* (New York: Harper, 1973), p. 154.

9. Stan Roberts, quoted in *Sunday Examiner and Chronicle* (San Francisco), 5 June 1977. Sec. A, p. 7.

10. John Boswell, in *News* (a United Methodist publication), 9 September 1975.

11. Matthew Poole, *Annotations on the Holy Bible* (1685, reprint ed., London: Banner of Truth, n.d.), p. 482.

12. John Albert Bengel, *Gnomon on the New Testament* (Edinburgh: T & T Clark, 1857), 3:22.

13. S. T. Bloomfield, *The Greek Testament, With English Notes* (London: Longmans, 1839), 2:10.

14. Thomas Aquinas, *Summa Theologica*, 2.2.154.11-12.

15. Ibid.

16. Boswell, *News*.

17. Dick Devor, in *Michigan Christian Advocate* (3 April 1975), pp. 11-12.

18. Ibid.

19. Alex Davidson, *The Returns of Love* (London: Inter-Varsity, 1971), p. 44.

### Chapter 3

1. Clement of Alexandria *Stromateis* 1.1.1.3.
2. Polycarp *To the Philippians* 5.3.
3. *The Teaching of the Twelve Apostles* 2.2
4. *The Epistle to Diognetus* 5.6-7.
5. Bardesanes *Book of the Laws of the Countries.*
6. Aristides *An Apology in Behalf of the Christians* 15.
7. Tatian *A Discourse to the Greeks* 38.
8. Ibid., 32.
9. Athenagoras *The Supplication for the Christians* 34.
10. Theophilus of Antioch *Ad Autolycum* 1.1
11. Ibid., 1.14.
12. Ibid., 3.15.
13. Clement *Stromateis* 3.18.109.
14. Origen *On Prayer* 29.13.
15. Ibid., 29.12.
16. Origen *The Dialogue With Heraclides* 150.2.443.
17. Athanasius *The Incarnation of the Word* 4.
18. Ibid., 5.
19. Inst. IV. xviii. 4.
20. Cod. Just. IX. ix. 31.
21. Johannes Quasten, *Patrology* (Utrecht: Spectrum, 1966), 3.429.
22. John Chrysostom, *Homilies on Romans,* IV.
23. Ibid.
24. Ibid.
25. Ibid.
26. Chrysostom *Homily II on 1 Timothy.*
27. Augustine *Sermon 161.*
28. Augustine *Sermon 162.*
29. Augustine *Sermon 163.*
30. Ibid.
31. Basil *God Is Not the Author of Evil,* 1, 2.
32. Basil *Letter 217.*

# Notes

33. Pelagius *On 1 Corinthians*.

34. Ambrosiaster *On 1 Timothy*.

35. Theodoret *On 1 Timothy*.

36. Theodoret *The Cure of Pagan Maladies or the Truth of the Gospels Proved From Greek Philosophy* 3.99.

37. Utrecht: Spectrum, 1966.

## Chapter 4

1. W. J. Gadpaille, "Research Into the Physiology of Maleness and Femaleness," *Archives of General Psychiatry* 26 (1972): 193-206.

2. R. V. Krafft-Ebing, *Psychopathia Sexualis* (Brooklyn: Physicians and Surgeons Book Company, 1933) pp. 335-52; Havelock Ellis, *Studies in the Psychology of Sex* (New York: Random, 1936), vol. 2, 2nd part, p. 74.

3. Gadpaille, "Maleness and Femaleness," p. 193.

4. R. Green, L. E. Newman, and R. J. Stoller, "Treatment of Boyhood Transsexualism," *Archives of General Psychiatry* 26 (1972): 213-17.

5. G. W. Harris, "Sex Hormones, Brain Development and Brain Function," *Endocrinology* 75 (1964): 627-48.

6. C. H. Phoenix et al., "Organizing Action of Prenatally Administered Testosterone Proprionate on the Tissues Mediating Maturing Behavior in the Female Guinea Pig," *Endocrinology* 65 (1959): 369-82.

7. Corinne Hutt, "Neuroendocrinological, Behavioral, and Intellectual Aspects of Sexual Differentiation in Human Development," in *Gender Differences: Their Ontogeny and Significance*, ed. C. Ounsted and D. C. Taylor (Baltimore: Williams, 1973), pp. 73-121.

8. J. Money, J. G. Hampson, and J. L. Hampson, "An Examination of Some Basic Sexual Concepts: The Evidence of Human Hermaphroditism," *Johns Hopkins Medical Journal* 97 (1955): 301-19.

9. D. B. Lynn, "A Note on Sex Differences in the Development of Masculine and Feminine Identification," *Psychological Review* 66 (1959): 126-35.

10. Gadpaille, "Maleness and Femaleness," p. 195.

11. See Hutt, "Sexual Differentiation," for a detailed bibliography.

12. Ibid., p. 112.

13. F. J. Kallman, "Comparative Twin Study on the Genetic Aspects

of Homosexuality," *Journal of Nervous and Mental Disease* 115 (1952): 283-98.

14. Gadpaille, "Maleness and Femaleness," pp. 197-200.

15. Ibid., p. 198. See also Gadpaille's comprehensive bibliography.

16. V. Halbreich, S. Segal, and I. Chowers, "Day to Day Variations in Serum Levels of Follicle-Stimulating Hormone and Luteinizing Hormone in Homosexual Males," *Biological Psychiatry* 13 (1978): 541-49.

17. P. G. Doerr et al., "Plasma Testosterone, Estradiol, and Semen Analysis in Male Homosexuals," *Archives of General Psychiatry* 29 (1973): 829-33; C. R. Kolodny et al., "Plasma, Gonadotropin and Prolactin in Male Homosexuals," *Lancet* 2 (1972): 18-20.

18. J. Loraine et al., "Patterns of Hormone Excretion in Male and Female Homosexuals," *Nature* 234 (1971): 552-55; C. R. Kolodny et al., "Plasma Testosterone and Semen Analysis in Male Homosexuals," *New England Journal of Medicine* 285 (1951): 1170-74.

19. C. J. Migeon, M. A. Rivarola, and M. G. Forrest, "Studies on Androgens in Transsexual Subjects: Effects of Estrogen Therapy," *Johns Hopkins Medical Journal* 123 (1968): 128-33.

20. L. Starka, I. Sipova, and J. Hynie, "Plasma Testosterone in Male Transsexuals and Homosexuals," *Journal of Sexual Research* 11 (1975): 134-38.

21. D. Barlow et al., "Plasma Testosterone Levels and Male Homosexuality: A Failure to Replicate," *Archives of Sexual Behavior* 3 (1974): 571-75; R. Pillard, R. Rose, and M. Sherwood, "Plasma Testosterone Levels in Homosexual Men," *Archives of Sexual Behavior* 3 (1974): 453-58; G. Tourney and L. Hatfield, "Androgen Metabolism in Schizophrenics, Homosexuals and Controls," *Biological Psychiatry* 6 (1973): 23-36; W. H. Masters and V. E. Johnson, *Homosexuality in Perspective*, (Boston: Little, Brown, 1979), pp. 409-11.

22. W. W. K. Zung and W. P. Wilson, "Response to Auditory Stimulation During Sleep,"*Archives of General Psychiatry* 4 (1961): 548-52.

23. W. P. Wilson, W. W. K. Zung, and J. C. M. Lee, "Arousal From Sleep of Male Homosexuals," *Biological Psychology* 6 (1973): 81-84.

24. Masters and Johnson, *Homosexuality in Perspective*, p. 142.

25. Gadpaille, "Maleness and Femaleness," p. 200.

26. G. Schmidt, V. Sigusch, and S. Schafer, "Responses to Reading

# Notes

Erotic Stories," *Archives of Sexual Behavior* 2 (1973): 181-99.

27. J. F. Oliven, *Sexual Hygiene and Pathology* (Philadelphia: Lippincott, 1955), p. 577.

28. S. Hadden, "Treatment of Male Homosexuals in Groups," *International Journal of Group Psychotherapy* 16 (1966), 13-22; E. Bergler, *Homosexuality: Disease or Way of Life*, (New York: Hill and Wang, 1957), pp. 188-89; C. W. Socarides, *The Overt Homosexual* (New York: Grune and Stratton, 1968), pp. 105-207; L. Hatterer, *Changing Homosexuality in the Male* (New York: McGraw-Hill, 1970), pp. 317-87; K. Freund, "Diagnosing Homo- or Hetero-Sexuality and Erotic Age Preference by Means of a Psychophysiological Test," *Behavior Research and Therapy* 5 (1967): 209-28.

29. C. W. Socarides, *The Overt Homosexual* (New York: Grune and Stratton, 1968), pp. 35-90; I. Bieber, *Homosexuality: A Psychoanalytic Study* (New York: Basic Books, 1962), pp. 1-207.

30. M. S. Weinberg and C. J. William, *Male Homosexuals: Their Problems and Adaptations* (New York: Penguin, 1975), p. 102.

31. J. Raboch and I. Sipova, "Intelligence in Homosexuals, Transsexuals, and Hypogonadotropic Eunuchoids," *Journal of Sexual Research* 10 (1974): 156-61.

32. T. G. Grygier, "Psychometric Aspects of Homosexuality," *Journal of Mental Science* 103 (1957): 514-26.

33. M. Siegelman, "Adjustment of Male Homosexuals and Heterosexuals," *Archives of Sexual Behavior* 2 (1972), 9-25; "Psychological Admustment of Homosexual and Heterosexual Men: A Gross National Replication," *Archives of Sexual Behavior* 7 (1978): 1-11.

34. Evelyn Hooker, "The Adjustment of the Male Overt Homosexual," *The Problem of Homosexuality in Modern Society*, ed. Hendrik M. Ruitbeek (New York: Dalton, 1963), pp. 141-61; "Male Homosexuals and Their Worlds," *Sexual Inversion: The Multiple Roots of Homosexuality*, ed. J. Marmor, (New York: Basic Books, 1965), pp. 83-107.

35. J. Marmor, "Homosexual and Sexual Orientation Disturbances," *Comprehensive Textbook of Psychiatry*, ed. A. M. Freedman, I. Kaplan, and B. J. Sadock (Baltimore: Williams, 1975), 1510-20.

36. I. Bieber, *Homosexuality: A Psychoanalytic Study* (New York: Basic Books, 1962), pp. 301-2; C. W. Socarides, *The Overt Homosexual* (New York: Grune and Stratton, 1968), pp. 105-207; Albert Ellis, "The Use of Psychotherapy with Homosexuals," *Mattachine Review* 2 (1956): 14-16; J. Marmor, "Notes on

Psychodynamic Aspects of Homosexuality," National Institute Mental Health Task Force on Homosexuality (Rockville, MD: National Institute of Mental Health, 1972).

37. J. C. Finney, "Homosexuality Treated With Combined Psychotherapy," *Journal of Social Therapy*, vol. 6, pp. 7-34; E. E. Mintz, "Overt Male Homosexuality in Combined Group and Individual Treatment," *Journal of Consult Psychology* 30 (1966): 193-98.

38. E. Glover, *The Roots of Crime: Selected Papers on Psychoanalysis*, vol. 2 (London: Imago, 1960), pp. 197-243.

39. C. W. Socarides, *The Overt Homosexual* (New York: Grune and Stratton, 1968), pp. 210-28.

40. Edmund Bergler, "Eight Prerequisites for the Psychoanalytic Treatment of Homosexuality," *Psychoanalytic Review* 31 (1944): 253-86.

41. S. B. Hadden, "Group Psychotherapy of Male Homosexuals," *Current Psychiatric Therapies* 6 (1966): 177-86.

42. J. D. Frank, "Treatment of Homosexuals," National Institute of Mental Health Task Force on Homosexuality (Rockville, MD: National Institute of Mental Health, (1972), pp. 63-68; A. B. Smith and A. Bassin, "Group Therapy with Homosexuals," *Social Therapy* 5 (1959): 225-32.

43. M. P. Feldman and M. J. MacCulloch, "The Application of Anticipatory Avoidance Learning to the Treatment of Homosexuality T. Theory, Technique and Preliminary Results," *Behavior Research and Therapy* 2 (1965): 165-83; Feldman et al., "The Application of Anticipatory Avoidance Learning to the Treatment of Homosexuality III. The Sexual Orientation Method," *Behavior Research and Therapy* 4 (1966): 289-99.

44. J. Srnge and K. Freund, "Treatment of Male Homosexuality Through Conditioning," *International Journal of Sexology* 7 (1953): 92-93.

45. Masters and Johnson, *Homosexuality in Perspective*, pp. 403-11.

46. W. P. Wilson and R. Abarno, "Christian and Homosexual: A Contradiction," *The Bulletin: Christian Association for Psychological Studies* 4 (1978): 21-24.

47. Masters and Johnson, *Homosexuality in Perspective*, pp. 1-411.

## Chapter 5

1. E. Carrington Boggan et al., *The Rights of Gay People: The Basic ACLU Guide to a Gay Person's Rights* (New York: Avon, 1975), p. 14.
2. McConnell v. Anderson, 316 F. Supp. 809, rev'd 451 F.2d 193 (1971).
3. *Constitutional Protection for Personal Life Styles*, 62 *Cornell Law Rev*. 563 (March 1977).
4. Arkansas Stat. Ann., sec. 41-813.
5. Arkansas Criminal Code, sec. 41-1801-1803.
5. *The Constitutionality of Laws Forbidding Private Homosexual Conduct*, 72 Michigan Law Rev. 1613 (August 1974).
7. Doe v. Commonwealth Attorney for City of Richmond, 403 F. Supp. 1199 (1975).
8. Norton v. Macy, 417 F.2d 1161 (1969); and Morrison v. State Board of Education, 82 Cal. Rptr. 175, 461 P.2d 375 (1969).
9. McConnell, 196.
10. Norton.
11. Richardson v. Hampton, 345 F. Supp. 600 (1972).
12. Safransky v. State Personnel Board, 62 Wis. 2d 464, 215 N. W. 2d 379.
13. *Homosexual's Legal Dilemma*, 27 Arkansas Law Rev. 687, 716 (Winter 1973).
14. Smith v. Liberty Mutual Insurance Co., 395 F. Supp. 1098 (1975).
15. Commonwealth v. Balthazar, 318 N. E. 2d 478 (1974); Posusta v. United States, 285 F.2d 533 (1969).
16. In re Labady, 326 F. Supp. 924, 930 (1971).

## Chapter 6

1. Barbara B. Gittings, "The Homophile Movement," in *The Same Sex*, ed. Ralph W. Weltge (Philadelphia: Pilgrim, 1969), p. 148.
2. Ibid., p. 149.
3. See John J. McNeill, *The Church and the Homosexual* (Kansas City: Sheed Andres and McMeel, 1976), pp. 172ff., for a brief statement of the purposes and position of these two organizations.
4. C. H. Patterson, *Theories of Counseling and Psychotherapy* (New York: Harper, 1973), pp. 10-11.

5. McNeill, *Church and Homosexual*, pp. 180-4.

6. Charles W. Socarides, "Homosexuality Is Not Just an Alternative Life Style," in *Male and Female*, ed. Ruth Tiffany Barnhouse and Urban T. Holmes, III (New York: Seabury, 1976), pp. 144-56.

7. From *Medical Aspects of Human Sexuality*, November 1977, quoted by Don Williams, "Shall We Revise the Homosexual Ethic?" *Eternity*, May 1978, p. 4.

8. Paul Chance, "Facts That Liberated the Gay Community," *Psychology Today* (December 1975), p. 52.

9. Several reviews of the report (Alan P. Bell and Martin S. Weinberg, *Homosexualities: A Study of Diversity Among Men and Women* [New York: Simon & Schuster, 1978]) have appeared in the media, including *Psychology Today*, August 1978; *Time*, 17 July 1978; and *The Courier-Journal* (Louisville, Kentucky), 16 July 1978.

10. Paul Tournier, "What Is Mental Health?" *McCormick Quarterly*, (November 1965), pp. 39-46, 52.

11. Ibid., p. 39.

12. Ibid., p. 43.

13. Ibid.

14. Ibid., p. 46.

15. Ibid., p. 45.

16. Ibid., p. 44.

17. Bennett J. Sims, "Sex and Homosexuality," *Christianity Today*, 24 February 1978, p. 26.

18. Ibid.

19. Paul Tourner, *The Healing of Persons* (New York: Harper, 1965), p. 183.

20. *Time* (17 July 1978), p. 53.

21. *Psychology Today* (August 1978), p. 53.

22. Alan Bell, "Homosexuality, an Overview," in *Male and Female*, ed. Ruth Tiffany Barnhouse and Urban T. Holmes, III (New York: Seabury, 1976), p. 139.

23. Walter H. Smartt, "Research Notes," *Family Life* (April 1972), p. 10.

24. R. D. Catterall, "Around the World," *Family Life* (August 1972), p. 6.

25. *Eternity* (February 1978), p. 12.

26. William Muehl, "Some Words of Caution," in *Male and Female,* ed. Ruth Tiffany Barnhouse and Urban T. Holmes, III (New York: Seabury, 1976), p. 169.

27. Ibid., pp. 171-72.

28. Ibid., p. 172.

29. Ibid., p. 172-73.

30. Alex Davidson, *The Returns of Love* (London: Inter-Varsity, 1971), p. 91.

31. Ibid.

32. Chance, "Facts," p. 55.

33. David F. Busby, "Sexual Deviations—A Psychiatric Overview," in *Proceedings of the Fourteenth Annual Convention of the Christian Association for Psychological Studies* (April 1967), pp. 55-60.

34. Bell, "Overview," pp. 141-42.

35. Davidson, *Returns.*

36. John Patton, "The View Point of the Pastor," in *Pastoral Psychology* (Spring 1976), p. 242.

37. Don S. Browning, *The Moral Context of Pastoral Care* (Philadelphia: Westminster, 1976). See also Perry London, *The Modes and Morals of Psychotherapy* (New York: Holt, Rinehart and Winston, 1964) and Paul W. Pruyser, *The Minister as Diagnostician* (Philadelphia: Westminster, 1976).

38. Norman Pittenger, "A Theological Approach to Understanding Homosexuality," in *Male and Female,* ed. Ruth Tiffany Barnhouse and Urban T. Holmes, III (New York: Seabury, 1976), p. 166.

39. *The Book of Discipline of the United Methodist Church,* (Nashville: United Methodist Publishing House, 1976), p. 110.

40. Ibid., pp. 110-11.

41. Ibid., p. 90.

42. McNeill, *Church and Homosexual,* p. 160.

43. Henri J. M. Nouwen, "The Self-availability of the Homosexual," in *Is Gay Good?* ed. W. Dwight Oberholtzer (Philadelphia: Westminster, 1971), pp. 204-12.

44. Ibid., p. 211.

45. See Jerry R. Kirk, *The Homosexual Crisis in the Mainline Church* (Nashville: Nelson, 1978), pp. 154-57 for additional suggestions along this line.

46. John F. Harvey, "Pastoral Responses to Gay World Questions," in *Is Gay Good?* ed. Oberholtzer, p. 136.

47. Ibid., p. 135.

48. Ibid., p. 137.

49. Ibid.

50. Howard Brown, *Familiar Faces, Hidden Lives*, quoted in *The Pastoral Counseling Review* (November 1976), p. 22.

51. John R. Powell, "Understanding Male Homosexuality: Developmental Recapitulation in a Christian Perspective," *Journal of Psychology and Theology* (Summer 1974), p. 168.

52. Lionel Ovesey, *Homosexuality and Pseudohomosexuality* (New York: Science, 1969).

53. Sims, "Sex and Homosexuality," p. 28.

54. McNeil, *Church and Homosexual*, p. 155.

55. H. Kimball Jones, *Toward a Christian Understanding of Homosexuality* (New York: Assoc. Press, 1966), p. 81.

56. Busby, "Sexual Deviations," p. 60.

57. J. Harold Greenlee, "Strawberry Blondes, Southpaws, and Civil Rights," *Good News* (November-December 1977), p. 42.

58. Jones, *Christian Understanding*, p. 102.

59. Paul Tournier, *To Understand Each Other* (Richmond: John Knox, 1967), p. 47.

60. Seward Hiltner, "Homosexuality: Psychological and Theological Perspectives," *Bulletin of the Christian Association of Psychological Studies*, vol. 3, no. 4 (1977), p. 2.

61. Mary S. Calderone, "Education for Heterosexuality," *The Journal of Pastoral Counseling* (Winter 1969-70), p. 9.

62. Ibid., p. 8.

63. Powell, "Understanding," p. 166.

64. Peter and Barbara Wyden, *Growing Up Straight* (New York: Stein and Day, 1968), p. 162.

# General Index

# General Index

Bieber, I., 159, 163, 193, 204-5, 211
Bill of Rights, 172
Biological cause (supposed) of homosexuality, 147, 157
Bisexuality, 215
Bisexuals, 166
Bloomfield, S. T., 99
Book of the Laws of the Countries (Bardesanes), 121
Boswell, John, 98-99, 101-2
Brazil, spiritism in, 31
Britain, 121; paedophilia in, 198
British law, 187
Brown, Howard, 214
Browning, Don, 207
Busby, David F., 204, 218
Byblos, 36

Caesarea, bishop of, 136
Cain and Abel, 53
Calderone, Mary S., 222
California, 218; University of, at Los Angeles, 188
California Personality Inventory, 160
Canaan, 54, 65-66
Canaanite(s), 36, 48-49; priests, 61
Capital punishment. See Death penalty.
Castaneda, Carlos, 25
Cataloqus Codicum Astrologorum Graecorum, 101
Catamite, 102
Catterall, R. D., 198
Celibacy, 83, 88-89, 93
Ceremonial law, 56-59, 61
Ceremonial uncleanness, 69
Chance, Paul, 189
Chesterton, G. K., 18
Childbearing, 63, 87. See also Procreation.
Child molestors, 178
Childs, Brevard, 75

Christ. See Jesus Christ.
Christian(s), 11, 14, 24, 46, 54, 62, 76, 89, 92, 96, 99, 102, 105, 107-13, 117-27, 134, 136ff., 164, 171-72, 184, 195, 211, 215, 225; church (see Church); college, 219; communities, 92, 123, 136, 142, 185, 221; Corinthian, 93; emperors, 129-30; ethic, 9, 125, 142, 199; gospel, 202, 224-25; heritage, 119; homosexual, 13, 167, 206, 223; life style, 120, 126, 138, 213; love (see Love); ministry to homosexuals, 183ff.; moral standards/values, 88, 102, 180; principles, 129, 167; reponsibility, 139, 175, 179; role in gay-rights controversy, 178-80; psychotherapy, 165; and sexuality, 88, 195, 222; viewpoint, 96, 109, 112, 122-23, 209, 221
Christianity, 17, 119-23, 127-29, 140-42
Chromosomal sex, 155
Chromosomes, 149, 151-53
Chrysostom, John, 131-35, 139
Church: aid to widows, 94; in Alexandria, 127; biblical warning to, 132; discipline within, 136-37; fathers (see Church fathers); homosexuality in, 9, 11; imperial politics in, 118; issues confronting, 124, 142; laws against homosexuality, 130; ministry to homosexuals, 183-225; pressures on, 179; response to homosexuality, 13, 117; sex education in, 221-23; sexual sin in, 133; synod, 127; teachers (see Church fathers)
Church fathers 71, 117-143
Cinaedus, 100
Civil justice, 69

240

# General Index

Eve, 41
Expositor's Greek New Testament, 90
Ezekiel, 24

Faith. See Jesus Christ, faith in.
Fall, the, 71, 192, 203
Family, 213, 223; dynamics and roles, 165, 167, 203; homosexuality a threat to, 132, 163; life, 132, 142; nuclear, in America, 173-75; preservation of, 87; relationships 84, 147
Fantasy patterns, 12, 166
Fathers, church. See Church fathers.
Fecundity, 66
Feldman, M. P., 163
Fellatio, 166
Female chromosomes, 149, 152-53
Female cult prostitutes, 64
Female hormones, 149ff.
Female vs. male development, 147ff.
Fertility cults, 38, 66
Fetus, 149, 153
Fidelity, 31, 117
Fifth Amendment, 174
First Amendment, 172, 174
Forgiveness, 108, 165, 215; theology of, 58
Fornication, 87-88, 91, 97-99, 107-8, 111, 122, 124, 135, 142
Fornicators, 99
Fourteenth Amendment, 172, 174-76, 180
Freud, Sigmund, 190, 204, 216
Freudian dynamic psychiatry, 147
Freudian psychoanalytic theory, 217
Freund, K., 163

Gadpaille, W. J., 147, 155, 157
Gamos, 95
"Gay Bob" dolls, 199
Gay: community, 11-13; liberation, 176; rights, 171ff.

Gender identity, 162
General Congress of the World Health Organization for Mental Health, 190
Genes, 151ff.
Genetic abnormalities, 155
Genetics, 148, 150ff., 167, 203
Genitalia, 149, 152, 155
Gentiles, 64
Gittings, Barbara B., 185
Glover, E., 163
Gnomon of the New Testament (Bengel), 99
God, 120-22; admonitions/commandments of, 121, 126; as Creator, 18, 34-36, 38, 40ff., 67-68, 75-76, 82, 100, 107, 112-13, 128, 131, 139, 147, 193; as Father, 39, 51; callings of, 194; character of, 18, 20-21, 33, 35-36, 39, 45, 49, 54-58, 60, 68, 75-76, 96, 107-8, 111-14, 122-23, 200; His claim on us, 112-14; estrangement from, 12, 133; faith in, 210, 225 (see also Jesus Christ, faith in); faithfulness of, 45, 49; gift of, 42, 47, 87, 107, 112, 135, 139, 183, 194-96, 202; grace of, 55, 85, 134-35, 210-11, 215, 223; image of, 17, 31, 85, 107, 125, 128, 136, 142, 195, 207; His intention for sex, 43, 109, 193; judgment of, 130, 132; law of, 24, 132; love of, 13, 24, 86, 212; obedience to, 20, 23, 124, 196; power of, 33, 35, 127; provision for sin, 57; His relation to humanity, 44; responsibility toward, 121, 193; roles of, 38-39; His self-revelation, 19-20, 69, 75; sin against, 104; Spirit of (see Holy Spirit); transcendence of, 32-38, 48-49, 53; will of, 64, 87, 104, 164, 191-94, 196; Word

# General Index

244

# General Index

# Scripture Index

# Scripture Index

# Scripture Index